Good Luck
Jim Messina

KEY

CORE

BELIEFS

KEY
CORE
BELIEFS

Unlocking the HEART of Happiness & Health

H. Gray Otis, PhD
Sandi Williams, MS, MA
James Messina, PhD

COLORIAN PRESS
Highland, Utah

COLORIAN PRESS
Highland, Utah 84003

Limit of Liability/Disclaimer of Warranty: While the authors have used their best efforts in preparing these materials, they make no representations or warranties with respect to the accuracy or completeness of the contents of this book and specifically disclaim any implied warranties of fitness for a particular purpose. No warranty may be created or extended by any representation of these materials. The ideas and strategies contained herein may not be suitable for a specific situation or for any set of circumstances. This work and its materials are designed to provide information of a general nature. The services of a competent professional should be sought if legal, accounting, medical, psychological, or any other expert assistance is required. This work is not intended as a substitute for the advice of healthcare professionals. Matters regarding a person's health require medical consultation with a physician as appropriate. Neither the publisher nor the authors shall be held liable for any loss or any damages allegedly arising from any information or materials in this book, including but not limited to special, incidental, consequential, or other damages.

Authors' Note: As licensed mental health professionals and as independent writers, we relied on research, personal experience, and professional observations to write this book. Although we have used expert opinions as resources, this book does not necessarily reflect any viewpoint or ideas except our own. This volume cites a number of individual accounts, but the names have been changed and the details of these accounts have been greatly altered to ensure anonymity. The concepts expressed in this volume may be used by licensed mental health professionals in their practice. However, no mental health professional or any other person may teach or present the concepts in this book or associated videos, programs, or materials to the public or other professionals unless certified by Key Core Beliefs, Inc. Certification requirements can be viewed online at KeyCoreBeliefs.org. Written certification will be furnished to each authorized provider.

H. Gray Otis, PhD, LCMHC, DCMHS-T, Licensed Clinical Mental Health Counselor
Sandi Williams, MS, MA, LMFT, Licensed Marriage and Family Therapist
James Messina, PhD, CCMHC, NCC, DCMHS-T, Licensed Psychologist

ISBN 978-1-7323658-0-3

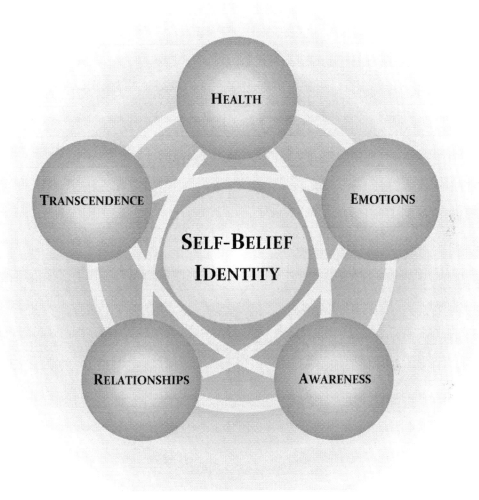

Very little is needed to make a happy life;
it is all within yourself, in your way of thinking.

Marcus Aurelius

With grateful acknowledgment for:
our loving marriage partners and our families,
our encouraging colleagues and those with whom we have worked,
our meticulous editor, Melinda Brown,
and our reviewing editor, Kathleen McCarthy,
and the grace that led us to our professional and personal passion
in the advancement of all-inclusive Core-Related Health.

CONTENTS

PREFACE

In the summer of 2016, the three of us—Gray, Sandi, and Jim—met to discuss concepts of health and emotional well-being that have guided our professional work as well our personal lives. Although Jim is a Licensed Psychologist, Sandi is a Licensed Marriage and Family Therapist, and Gray is a Licensed Clinical Mental Health Counselor, our approach to counseling is remarkably similar. We decided to join together to share our perception that the power of Key Core Beliefs combined with Health Integration can be life-changing.

These concepts have proven to be a highly effective means for the three of us to increase our own Core-Related Health. We continually apply the ideas of this book in our personal lives because they work for us. This has been also true for many individuals and couples with whom we have worked. We have seen how these concepts of health wellness, mental and emotional well-being, greater transcendence, and enriched relationships change lives. We are convinced everyone could benefit from these concepts.

This book draws on a variety of ideas from many disciplines. We hope you will discover a richer, more complete approach to living with greater enjoyment and fulfilment. To this end, "KEY CORE BELIEFS" is dedicated to you.

H. Gray Otis, PhD, LCMHC, Licensed Clinical Mental Health Counselor
Sandi Williams, MS, MA, LMFT, Licensed Marriage and Family Therapist
James Messina, PhD, CCMHC, NCC, DCMHS-T, Licensed Psychologist

HOW THIS BOOK WILL CHANGE YOUR LIFE

In the pages of this book, you will meet a number of people and learn some of their deepest struggles and secrets. Most of these individuals had given up all hope that their lives could change for the better.

We're sharing their stories because their problems are ones that many others have faced. However, we are also telling their stories because all of these individuals have used the approaches in this book to create successful lives with greater enjoyment and satisfaction. You will meet:

❑ *Gerrit*, who discovered how his hidden fear that he was stupid was sabotaging his relationship with his wife.

❑ *Andrea*, whose marriage and health were failing because of the demands of her job and the unresolved distress of prior painful experiences.

❑ *Shelley*, who was convinced that she was forever trapped by her own disastrous decisions.

❑ *Jeremy*, who despite his many achievements and wonderful family relationships, had been depressed for years because he thought of himself as a disappointment.

These and the other stories you will read in this book illustrate how each of us can come to better understand ourselves and the people who mean the most to us. As our self-awareness increases, we can greatly improve how we experience our lives. We can also build a deeper sense of self-worth as well as greater happiness and health.

How we create true success

The foundation of all real success is based on our Core-Related Health, which comprehensively combines our physical wellness (our health) with our emotional well-being (our mental health).

The two fundamentals of total Core-Related Health are shown in the following box:

THE FUNDAMENTALS OF CORE-RELATED HEALTH

☐   A Self-Belief Identity based on Positive Core Beliefs

☐   The five essentials of Health Integration

Complete physical wellness and emotional well-being
only occur when these fundamentals are combined.

These two fundamentals are mutually supportive and highly interconnected. They completely shape our ability to achieve more enjoyment and satisfaction. A Self-Belief Identity based on our Key Core Beliefs is discussed in Chapter 1, and the five essentials of Health Integration are discussed in Chapter 2.

Unfortunately, most of us do not understand how the basics of Core-Related Health impact every aspect of our lives. In addition, many medical and mental health professionals may not grasp how these two fundamentals intricately work together to promote wellness, a buoyant sense of identity, more positive relationships, and an added sense of personal purpose. In fact, Health Integration and Self-Belief Identity go hand-in-hand to create who we are. Together, they decisively help us respond to life's challenges and opportunities.

A Self-Belief Identity based on Positive Core Beliefs and Health Integration forms a conceptualization of comprehensive health for individuals and families. Each of us can create happier and healthier lives by learning how to put into practice both of these fundamentals.

In Chapter 1, Gerrit's story demonstrates how Positive Core Beliefs lead to the development of the first fundamental, our Self-Belief Identity. The story of Andrea in Chapter 2 illustrates how the other fundamental, Health Integration, produces total Core-Related Health. Chapter 3 reviews how our relationships are vital to the development of both our Key Core Beliefs and Self-Belief Identity. Shelly's story shows how this happens. The other chapters discuss how to use our Key Core Beliefs to create more enjoyment and meaning.

This book is based on the clinical observations of the authors in their work with thousands of individuals. It focuses on ideas that have been instrumental for many to create a constructive Self-Belief Identity and a healthier approach to wellness and well-being. Although each of the authors has engaged in research, there is no intent to present this book as a scientific study. And while the authors cannot ensure that these ideas will be successful for every personal set of circumstances, we invite every reader to consider whether the concepts in this book could be personally beneficial.

In order to assure confidentiality, the personal stories and names of the individuals in this book have been changed so that the accounts do not directly link to any specific person or situation.

REVIEW ACTIVITIES

At the end of 11 of the 12 chapters in the book, you'll find review activities that we encourage you to consider doing. They will enrich your understanding and application of the ideas presented in this book.

Click on the Activities tab at KeyCoreBeliefs.org to print out the Chapter Review Activities. Under the Activities tab you will also find links to additional activities that are available without cost.

DEFINITION OF TERMS

Major ideas presented in "KEY CORE BELIEFS" are defined below.

TERM	DEFINITION
Key Core Beliefs	Strongly held self-beliefs (e.g., "I am competitive") that shape our perceptions, thoughts, emotions, and behaviors.
Positive Core Beliefs	Key Core Beliefs based on productive or beneficial experiences that strengthen an accurate and favorable self-identity (e.g., "I am considerate").
Negative Core Beliefs	Key Core Beliefs based on problematic or harmful experiences that strengthen an inaccurate and unfavorable self-identity (e.g., "I am helpless").
Self-Belief Identity	The profound sense of who we are—our unique individuality—based on our accumulated Key Core Beliefs (e.g., "I am considerate but often I am resentful and I am helpless to change").
Health Integration	The integration of all health essentials—physical, mental, emotional, transcendent, and relational.
Core-Related Health	The two fundamentals of wellness and well-being: ❑ A Self-Belief Identity primarily based on Positive Core Beliefs, and ❑ Health Integration
Mental Health Professional	A licensed psychotherapist or counselor with at least a master's degree, who is trained to diagnose and treat psychological disorders. These include: ❑ Licensed Clinical Mental Health Counselors ❑ Licensed Professional Counselors ❑ Licensed Marriage and Family Therapists ❑ Licensed Clinical Social Workers ❑ Licensed Psychologists ❑ Licensed Nurse Practitioners ❑ Physician Assistants trained in psychiatry ❑ Licensed Psychiatrists

The terms Key Core Beliefs™, Positive Core Beliefs™, Negative Core Beliefs™, Self-Belief Identity™, and Core-Related Health™ are trademarked.

Section One

DISCOVERING
THE FUNDAMENTALS
OF CORE-RELATED
HEALTH

BUILDING
KEY CORE BELIEFS

Making Sense of Our Experiences

The only person you are destined
to become is the person
you decide to be.

Ralph Waldo Emerson

WHAT ARE SELF-BELIEFS AND WHY ARE THEY IMPORTANT?

What we strongly believe about ourselves is the most crucial characteristic of our lives. These self-beliefs greatly influence each perception of our experiences, all of our feelings and thoughts, and every action we take. Some of these beliefs are conscious while others lie below the surface of our awareness. Each person has hundreds of interrelated self-beliefs. Understanding these beliefs can improve every aspect of who we are.

Our self-beliefs can be changed. They can become much more beneficial. The ability to transform our beliefs continues throughout our lifetime. If we desire to become happier, healthier, or more successful, the roadmap for positive change begins with our incredible capacity to alter our self-beliefs. These results can be remarkable.

WE ARE WHAT WE BELIEVE

For decades, people have debated the relative importance of "genetics verses environment" or "nature verses nurture," and which most influences our thinking and behavior. That issue may never be fully resolved; however, there is no question that our accumulated self-beliefs meaningfully impact every part of our lives.

For example, an individual who has achieved a measure of success in sports, in a profession, or in any other endeavor will persistently work towards continued success. That person would think to themselves, "Hey, I'm good at this!" By contrast, someone who repeatedly experiences personal disappointments might lose motivation and ultimately stop pursuing a previously desired objective. He or she might believe, "No matter what I do, I am always ineffective—it's hopeless." These are examples of self-beliefs.

Our accumulated experiences are linked to our ongoing, internal dialogue—our self-talk. Even in the midst of talking with a friend, we continue this dialogue. We determine what we are going to say next—and not say—and have many other thoughts that may or may not apply to what is being talked about. Most of our thought processes are actually conversational stories within our cognitive mind.

The vast majority of this internal dialogue is never revealed to others. As this dialogue accumulates, it contributes to what we believe about others. Much more decisively, our self-talk crucially determines what we believe about ourselves.

Defining Key Core Beliefs

Key Core Beliefs are powerfully held beliefs about who we are. These beliefs are descriptions about ourselves that we presume to be true. They affect our physical wellness and emotional well-being because these beliefs shape our perceptions, thoughts, emotions, and behaviors.

For example, most famous comics realized at a young age that they had a talent for making others laugh, which gave them a sense that they were good at amusing others. Many were encouraged to increase their comedic talents. They developed a Key Core Belief, "I am funny."

Conversely, if a child who tried to be humorous were told that he or she was stupid or flippant, the child would be much less likely to use humor to connect with others. He or she might mistakenly believe, "I am not funny" or "I am boring."

KEY CORE BELIEFS

Key Core Beliefs are strongly held convictions about ourselves that are vital to our physical wellness and emotional well-being. These self-beliefs shape our perceptions, thoughts, emotions, and behaviors.

Each of us has a great many Key Core Beliefs. It's important to be aware of these beliefs because they help us understand how we perceive and respond to our experiences. In addition, they interrelate with all aspects of our lives. What we believe about our HEALTH, our EMOTIONS, our AWARENESS, our RELATIONSHIPS, and our

TRANSCENDENCE greatly impacts how we view ourselves. For example, if a person has a Key Core Belief that "I am not enough," this will significantly impact the individual's perceptions, feelings, thoughts, and actions.

However, many of the beliefs we have about ourselves are untrue. Some self-beliefs may be based on mistaken interpretations of our experiences. The following story illustrates how a Key Core Belief can be incorrect. Gerrit was having a difficult time with his marriage partner. This troubled him so much that he decided to talk to his friend, Frank, a mental health professional.

GERRIT'S STORY

One day I was talking to Frank and I told him I had recently been feeling on edge and more irritated. However, I couldn't identify what was pushing my buttons. How do you talk about a problem if you don't know what's bothering you? Frank said he thought an underlying Key Core Belief was troubling me. He was convinced I could identify the belief, and he asked me what had been going on when I was irritated. For several minutes, I talked about little issues that seemed to be more of a problem to me than I thought they ought to be. Nevertheless, I could not identify any underlying belief.

It was a frustrating experience for me and it seemed our conversation was going nowhere, but Frank persisted. In the midst of my exasperation, I started to talk about a series of interactions with my partner. I said that sometimes when we were talking, she'd make comments to me that were so patently obvious it seemed as though she was talking to a child. These remarks annoyed me and I frequently responded by saying, "Why would you say that? Do you think I'm stupid?" As soon as I said that, it was immediately clear—my troubling Key Core Belief was, "I am stupid."

I began to realize how this belief had been lurking in the back of my mind for many years. As I became more aware of this, I realized that similar negative thoughts about myself came up quite often. For example, if I made a mistake, I would say to myself, "Gerrit, you're such an idiot!" Often, I remembered the comment of a high school girlfriend who told me more than once, "You're not too bright, Gerrit." It was said as a joke, but those words stuck with me.

As I discussed these thoughts with Frank, he asked if I thought this belief was true. "Of course not," I said. However, I remember what a struggle it had been for me to get good grades in school. My folks were constantly telling me I could do better. Other problems also contributed to my belief that I wasn't too bright. If my wife reminded me to do something, I felt dumb for not remembering. When others gave me directions, I thought I should have known better. Every mistake I made was evidence that there was something wrong with me.

As I talked this out with Frank, it became more apparent that my "stupidity" was not true. Yes, I made mistakes, but I learned from them. Instead of getting down on myself, I changed how I reacted to these experiences. Before long, I could clearly recognize when I was criticizing myself and I could replace my self-criticism with the more accurate belief, "I am smart and I am learning."

Because I was able to change the pattern of these thoughts, I became more self-assured. Although sometimes I may humorously question the level of my intelligence, I never reinforce it with the question, "Do you think I am stupid?" Not surprisingly, this has made a positive difference for both me and my partner.

Gerrit's story illustrates the power of Key Core Beliefs. These self-beliefs can exist consciously or subconsciously. A conscious belief may be repeatedly reinforced. For example, a woman said, "Ever since I was a little girl, I have believed, 'I am a late bloomer.' As a child, I was stubborn. Even though I had more trouble learning to ride a bike and master the multiplication tables than other children, I was convinced that if I persisted in an effort, I would be successful—but only after everyone else. Even now, I continue to believe, 'I may be slow but I will succeed in spite of myself." Her comments demonstrate how conscious Key Core Beliefs, such as, "I am a late bloomer" and "I am persistent," can be strengthened by repetition.

Often however, our self-beliefs lie below the surface of the conscious mind as seen in Gerrit's story. They can be discovered, but it sometimes takes a little effort to bring them to conscious awareness. When we are aware of our Key Core Beliefs, we can determine if they are accurate or inaccurate beliefs. If any of them prove to be untrue, it is possible to change these self-beliefs.

Some beliefs are much more important than others and create a very strong sense of who we are. One person who had a healthy childhood was afflicted with diabetes in his mid-teens. When he was asked about some of his most significant self-beliefs, he immediately replied, "I was well, but now I am sick. That changed everything." In contrast, another individual who was paralyzed due to a car accident said, "This wheelchair doesn't define me. As far as I'm concerned, I am healthy."

POSITIVE AND NEGATIVE CORE BELIEFS

It is crucial to learn to recognize whether a Key Core Belief is favorable or unfavorable. If a self-belief is constructive, we refer to it as a Positive Core Belief. Our favorable beliefs are based on productive or beneficial experiences. They strengthen an accurate and positive sense of self (e.g., "I am considerate"). As we shall see, these beliefs help us create enjoyable and worthwhile future events.

On the other hand, if a Key Core Belief is inaccurate or detrimental, we refer to it as a Negative Core Belief. These beliefs are based on problematic, harmful, or disadvantageous experiences. They strengthen a false or unfavorable sense of self (e.g., "I am helpless"). Negative Core Beliefs generally create undesirable perceptions, feelings, thoughts, and behaviors that result in poor outcomes. For example, if someone believes, "I never measure up, I'm so brainless," over time he or she will become more convinced that this Negative Core Belief is accurate.

It is important to become aware of our negative beliefs and then replace them with Positive Core Beliefs. When we do this, we enhance both our personal and interpersonal effectiveness.

To illustrate this, let's refer to Gerrit's prior belief, "I am stupid." Before he could positively deal with this Negative Core Belief, he had to first bring this belief to his conscious awareness. Only then could he be mindful of how this conviction was influencing his life in ways that created unnecessary problems.

After becoming aware of this belief, he was then able to catch himself in his thoughts and avoid negatively reacting. He learned how to be more mindful of situations when he felt inadequate. His increased awareness gave him the opportunity to acknowledge his competence as he dealt with challenging experiences.

At the same time, he was changing his previous Negative Core Belief to a more accurate and favorable Positive Core Belief, "I am capable." He later said that he never again said to his wife, "Do you think I am stupid?" Gerrit's old self-belief no longer haunted him.

Positive Core Beliefs strengthen a constructive and desirable sense of self. They develop through favorable, supportive, or effective experiences. For example:

"I have demonstrated over and over again that others can rely on me."

The Positive Core Belief is, "I am reliable."

In contrast, Negative Core Beliefs support an undesirable sense of self. They develop through ineffective, harmful, or problematic experiences. For example:

"No matter what I do, terrible things keep happening to me."

The Negative Core Belief is, "I am helpless to stop this" or "I am helpless."

We often presume our Negative Core Beliefs are accurate because there is usually some element of truth to them. Like Gerrit, at times we all do not fully understand some events or the meaning of someone's comments. Of course, this does not mean we are stupid. However, when we give too much credence to these experiences, the power of our Negative Core Beliefs increases. When this occurs, our Negative Core Beliefs gain influence over our conscious and subconscious mental processes, just as Gerrit's story demonstrated.

Every one of us has a number of Core Beliefs; however, Negative Core Beliefs often play a disproportionate role in our sense of self. To illustrate this, many of us have no difficulty listing several of our negative qualities, but we find it very challenging to list even a few of our positive qualities. Most of us are quite critical of ourselves. These undesirable interpretations about ourselves often create an unrealistic and unfavorable sense of who we are.

RECOGNIZING NEGATIVE CORE BELIEFS

Each person's experiences are uniquely interwoven into related patterns of Positive Core Beliefs and similar patterns of Negative Core Beliefs. Our personal stories include a tapestry of linked memories, thoughts, and emotions. Each significant event has meaning for us, and these important life stories relate to one or more of our self-beliefs. As we tell the stories of our lives, our Key Core Beliefs can be recognized and understood.

To identify your own Key Core Beliefs, perhaps the best place to start is to identify any Negative Core Beliefs that have become a part of how you see yourself. To illustrate, take a look at the list of beliefs below. Try to determine if you have ever had one or more of these. See if you still deal with any of them. As you review this brief list of beliefs, note if any other Negative Core Beliefs come to your mind.

EXAMPLES OF NEGATIVE CORE BELIEFS

"I am not too smart."	"I am never good enough."
"I am always anxious."	"I am hopeless."
"I am a mess."	"I don't deserve love"
"I am damaged."	"I am stupid."
"I am a disappointment."	"I am out of control."
"I am a goofball."	"I am a jerk."
"I am an idiot."	"I am fat."
"I am ugly."	"I am wrong."
"I am dishonest."	"I am boring."
"I am untrusting of others."	"I cannot trust myself."
"I am unsafe."	"I am a coward."
"I am depressed."	"I am sick."
"I am a people pleaser."	"I am slow."
"I am a quitter."	"I am not myself."
"I am thoughtless."	"I am selfish."
"I am undeserving."	"I am helpless."
"I am weak."	"I am immoral."
"I am unreliable."	"I am a loser."

"I am a failure."

"I cannot please others."

"I am fickle."

"I am uncontrollable."

"I don't belong" or "I am weird."

"Others would be better off without me."

"I should have known."

"I am never going to change."

"I don't measure up."

"I don't matter."

"I am incompetent."

"I am never good enough."

"I am such a pain."

"I am invisible."

"I am garbage."

"I am worthless."

"I am inadequate."

"I am not lovable."

When we become aware of these or any other adverse beliefs, we are then able to understand ourselves more completely. For many of us, this helps us figure out why we have acted in ineffective or harmful ways that never made any sense to us. We can also begin to see how many of our Negative Core Beliefs are linked to previous events. Know that these experiences can be resolved—we can learn how to transform undesirable beliefs into Positive Core Beliefs.

Here's how one woman described this process:

"When I looked back on my angry outbursts towards my husband, they never made any sense. I'd get mad over really trivial things. Afterwards, my anger seemed kind of stupid. Of course, I always blamed him for making me angry. It was not until I recognized my own Negative Core Beliefs that I understood how they were always at the root of my anger. Only then could I begin the process of healing myself and creating a much better partnership. I did this when I learned how to exchange my old beliefs for Positive Core Beliefs."

Mental health professionals rarely see people who have predominantly Positive Core Beliefs. These individuals have a constructive sense of who they are, which enables them to work through challenges. They generally enjoy their lives.

However, individuals with mental disorders regularly talk about their Negative Core Beliefs. For instance, if a person says, "I am anxious," he or she will often mention a number of other self-critical beliefs. Mental health professionals who understand the underlying causes of mental illness can support individuals as they transform their Negative Core Beliefs into more accurate Positive Core Beliefs. Unsurprisingly, this usually alleviates or eliminates related symptoms such as depression or anxiety.

THE ACCUMULATION OF KEY CORE BELIEFS

We all have numerous Key Core Beliefs. We do not know how many of these beliefs we have because a large number of our beliefs lie below our conscious awareness. They include self-beliefs about our values, culture, race, nationality, sexuality, gender, politics, education, etc. In addition, these beliefs filter our perceptions, govern our emotions, guide our thoughts, and shape how we act. They organize what we do and how we interact with others.

These beliefs accumulate over the course of our lives. When combined, these self-beliefs create our sense of who we are—our Self-Belief Identity.

SELF-BELIEF IDENTITY

Our Self-Belief Identity is the profound sense of who we are—our unique individuality—and it is primarily based on many of our most important Key Core Beliefs. We can create a favorable Self-Belief Identity when we ensure that most of the beliefs we have about ourselves are constructive, Positive Core Beliefs.

Because Key Core Beliefs so persuasively influence us, they are central to how we see ourselves. Every new experience is filtered through the lens of our identity and our self-beliefs. This enables us to organize our experiences and make conclusions about who we are. Our Key Core Beliefs and Self-Belief Identity help us understand ourselves, and they are also essential to how we perceive others. Our Self-Belief Identity creates patterns of accruing experiences over time and enables us to make sense of our interactions with others.

For example, adult siblings may react to each other in predictable ways based on their childhood experiences and the beliefs they formed about themselves. If one sibling periodically mistreated another, the mistreated one may still believe as an adult, "I am unsafe with my sibling" or "I am weak," etc. To become more effective in our interactions with others, it is crucial to know how our Key Core Beliefs impact us.

USING POSITIVE CORE BELIEFS TO CREATE A CONSTRUCTIVE SELF-BELIEF IDENTITY

Each person is different from all others. We have a distinctive combination of inherited traits and exclusive experiences that are greatly influenced by our relationships. Our traits, our experiences, our relationships, and our Key Core Beliefs create a one-of-a-kind individual. Literally, there never has been and never will be any person who is exactly like us.

As part of our human capabilities, we have the ability to change our Negative Core Beliefs. By understanding them, we can convert them to desirable beliefs. As we will learn in the third chapter, we can use the development of Positive Core Beliefs to strengthen our Self-Belief Identity. To summarize:

- ❑ Key Core Beliefs influence our perceptions, feeling, thoughts, and behaviors.
- ❑ Each Key Core Belief is either a Positive Core Belief or Negative Core Belief.
- ❑ All of these beliefs combine to create our Self-Belief Identity.
- ❑ We have the ability to transform any Negative Core Belief into a Positive Core Belief.
- ❑ When most of our self-beliefs are Positive Core Beliefs, we develop a constructive Self-Belief Identity.

Our Self-Belief Identity is the first of the two fundamentals of Core-Related Health. In the next chapter, we discuss the second fundamental—Health Integration. We will discover how the five essentials of wellness and emotional well-being play a crucial role in increasing our Positive Core Beliefs. The later chapters discuss how our other Key Core Beliefs can progressively create enhanced relationships, added enjoyment, and healthier lives.

REVIEW ACTIVITY
Chapter 1

Most of us deal with significant challenges throughout our lives. Many relate to our accumulated Key Core Beliefs. When we successfully overcome a problem, it usually means we have strengthened a Positive Core Belief. For example, a belief might have been, "I am not coordinated enough to play sports." In contrast, if a person trained hard and completed a long run, a tough bike ride, or an extended swim, the Core Belief could become, "I am athletic in endurance events."

Before moving on to Chapter 2, consider the following ideas:

EXERCISE: Are You Aware of Your Core Beliefs?

Can you identify three of your Positive Core Beliefs?

Now, can you identify three Negative Core Beliefs?

What can you learn about yourself based on the Positive and Negative Core Beliefs you have identified?

You can print out each Chapter Review Activity under the Activities tab at KeyCoreBeliefs.org. At the end of most of the Chapter Review Activities, you'll find a link to additional activities that are available without cost.

NOTES: Use this page to record any thoughts about Key Core Beliefs, Positive Core Beliefs or Negative Core Beliefs, and Self-Belief Identity.

THE HEART
OF HEALTH INTEGRATION

Achieving Greater Health & Well-Being

*Courage is knowing
what not to fear.*

Plato

HOW CAN WE ACHIEVE HEALTH INTEGRATION?

Health Integration is fundamental because it incorporates the five essentials of physical wellness and emotional well-being: HEALTH, EMOTIONS, AWARENESS, RELATIONSHIPS, and TRANSCENDENCE. In order to be healthy and well-adjusted, we cannot afford to overlook any of these quality-of-life necessities. Together they regulate our overall health and simultaneously strengthen our Positive Core Beliefs. Andrea's story illustrates this.

ANDREA'S STORY

Andrea was stuck in a job that was too demanding and a marriage that was deteriorating. After six years of dealing with chronic worry, she developed a drinking problem that was getting worse. Her anxiety and drinking combined with the normal stress of a tough marketing job reduced her ability to resist infections. The tipping point came when a winter cold turned into violent coughing and a trip to an urgent-care health facility. She was diagnosed with viral pneumonia and immediately hospitalized.

During her second day in the hospital, Andrea's attending physician and nurse reviewed her health history and with her permission acquired her electronic health records. As part of her overall evaluation, a mental health professional, working in the hospital as a behavioral health consultant, also spent some time with Andrea. Together, these three professionals then considered several factors that contributed to her health concerns.

❑ Her immune system was compromised. The pneumonia as well as other viral infections had increased over the past three years. In addition, in the last 12 months, she had had a growing number of major headaches.

❑ Andrea was also dealing with chronic distress related to her worsening relationship with her husband, Gabe. She said that they had a lot of arguments. After their fights, they often withdrew from each other and sometimes did not speak for days. Andrea said she regularly was the loser in these conflicts. She also expressed a significant degree of resentment towards Gabe.

❑ Her work was disrupted by a series of crises brought about by constantly changing work requirements. Although she worked with a team of supportive individuals, she believed her performance was never quite up to the expectations of her supervisor.

> ❑ She used drinking to cope with her chronic anxiety and depression but it had increased considerably. Two years ago, Andrea had a single glass of wine at dinner. Now, she routinely drank three glasses of wine in the evenings. She said she consumed even more on the weekends.
>
> ❑ Andrea completed a brief questionnaire that reviewed upsetting experiences during her childhood and teen years. Based on her answers, it was apparent that she had unresolved trauma related to high school sexual harassment. This past distress was playing out in the present because she was convinced that she had a "weak personality." This Negative Core Belief was self-evident since she could never "say no" to the demands of others.
>
> All of these factors were combining to create a sense of inadequacy. When Andrea was asked to summarize her life in one sentence, she quickly replied, "I am such a failure!"

Andrea's health issues were all interrelated. Her compromised immune system related to the pressures of the ever-changing demands at work as well as her difficult marriage. Her growing alcohol consumption was used as an ineffective coping mechanism to dull her troubles. However, it also reduced her ability to resist infections. In addition, the traumatic teenage bullying was contributing to her personal and professional problems, but Andrea had no idea that the bullying was a factor. All of these issues were taking a toll on her physical wellness, her emotional well-being, and her marriage.

If Andrea had not received this level of comprehensive assessment, her doctor might have treated the pneumonia and then released her from the hospital. Without total healthcare, she would have likely faced continuing medical concerns, ongoing marital conflicts, increased alcohol use, and possibly other problems.

Fortunately, Andrea had a team of both medical specialists and mental health professionals who were passionate about the essentials of complete health. These professionals worked together to ensure the total wellness and well-being of those entrusted to their care. Health Integration was the standard of treatment at this hospital.

COMPREHENSIVE HEALTH

What was the impact of Health Integration for Andrea? She worked with her health care team, including Margo, a mental health professional, to create a comprehensive treatment plan. This plan helped her gain greater control and increased responsibility for her health. To effectively address her health concerns, the following approach was devised:

❑ After treating the pneumonia, Andrea learned how to increase the strength of her immune system by paying attention to health practices that included:

◊ Improved dietary guidelines with a focus on nutritious eating.

◊ Increased hours of sleep from her previous average of five hours to at least seven hours per night through the application of sleep hygiene routines.

◊ Augmented hydration by decreasing her caffeine consumption and increasing the amount of water she consumed.

◊ Added physical activity through daily walks of 20 minutes or more.

❑ With added sleep, improved hydration, reduced intake of caffeine, better nutrition, and increased physical activity, her headaches became significantly less severe and less frequent. When she did have a headache, it was effectively managed by meditation, cool compresses, and one or two aspirin.

❑ Although her work circumstances could not be altered, Margo helped Andrea to develop better strategies for successfully getting through the work day. These included hourly, two-minute breaks from work such as brief chats with supportive co-workers and mini-walks within her building. Additionally, through assertiveness training she learned how to inform her supervisor that needless work changes were impeding her performance. Gradually, she began to feel more confident and less stressed.

❑ By confronting her alcohol use, Andrea began to understand why increased drinking was a poor choice for coping with her stress. With Margo's assistance, she learned to recognize her alcohol cravings and to substitute positive coping skills such as eating a healthy snack or talking with a friend. She also met others who had had problems with drinking, attended 12 Step meetings, and enlisted the help of a sponsor. Also, Andrea and Gabe discovered new ways to connect with each other, such as going for an evening walk together.

❏   Although Andrea told Margo that she had been sexually taunted by another girl during her freshman and sophomore years in high school, she was unaware that these teenage experiences were related to her health issues, her chronic worrying, her drinking, and her partner conflicts. As she worked with her counselor, who was a specialist in trauma resolution, she was able to resolve these concerns. For years, Andrea had the Negative Core Belief, "I am a weak person." This harmful belief and others were transformed into Positive Core Beliefs.

❏   Margo also worked with Gabe and Andrea together. As a couple, they found productive ways to deal with their differences. They also discovered how effectively regulating their emotions could help them successfully manage their feelings. By developing the crucial skill of empathy, they began to understand each other more fully and were able to positively work through their problems.

Andrea's story illustrates the tremendous value of Health Integration. Successfully recovering from many physical problems requires more than just medical care alone. When she was admitted to the hospital, the comprehensive review of Andrea's health highlighted how her lack of behavioral well-being had contributed to a compromised immune system and pneumonia. Without holistic assessment and treatment, Andrea would have most likely faced continuing health problems, mental and emotional issues, and a struggling relationship.

The benefits of Health Integration rely on five essentials. All of us can learn how to better develop these essentials. Our exploration will demonstrate how to develop more comprehensive health wellness and greater emotional well-being.

THE FIVE ESSENTIALS OF HEALTH INTEGRATION

Andrea's story illustrates that a complete approach to wellness and well-being is not achieved through partial answers or simplistic solutions. Overall health can only be attained when we pay attention to the five Health Integration essentials:

THE ESSENTIALS OF HEALTH INTEGRATION

HEALTH—physical wellness based on the principles of healthy living

EMOTIONS—emotional balance through self-understanding

AWARENESS—conscious use of our mental abilities

RELATIONSHIPS—caring and satisfying connections with others

TRANSCENDENCE—enrichment through inspiring and uplifting influences

The first letters of these five essentials—HEALTH, EMOTIONS, AWARENESS, RELATIONSHIPS, and TRANSCENDENCE—are referred to by the acronym HEART™. They all interact with each other in mutually supportive or mutually disruptive ways. When these essentials are predominantly detrimental, we are more likely to face problematic concerns that increase our negative beliefs about who we are. When these essentials are primarily constructive, we become more resilient, develop richer relationships, and reinforce positive beliefs about ourselves.

Additionally, if one of these health components deteriorates, the other four areas will often be adversely affected. For example, inadequate sleep impacts our physical HEALTH, but it also creates problems with our EMOTIONS, our AWARENESS and cognitive functioning, as well as our RELATIONSHIPS and our ability to feel connected. As was the case with Andrea, physical health and mental health concerns are interrelated in every aspect of our lives. The five HEART essentials of Health Integration help us understand how to achieve a greater degree of physical wellness, emotional well-being, life satisfaction, and enjoyment.

DEVELOPING HEALTH INTEGRATION

Most of us know individuals who are passionate about their physical fitness. These people always take the stairs instead of the elevator, they don't eat a lot of sugary foods, and they manage to work out or stay physically active every day regardless of the demands on their time. These people may be physically healthy, but some of them may struggle to make and keep friends. Others may be completely overwhelmed by the thought of dealing with their own emotions. Still others may have concerns about their mental abilities or they may believe they are not as intelligent as they want to be.

We can increase our overall Health Integration when we recognize and develop each of the five HEART essentials. As we optimize our overall health, we live more fully. This holistic approach is also vitally important to our sense of who we are. Each of the five essentials contributes to our Key Core Beliefs and significantly strengthens our Self-Belief Identity.

When we develop more Positive Core Beliefs through Health Integration practices, we can shape our lives in the ways that we want them to unfold. We may not solve every problem, but we will face our issues with greater clarity and confidence. The results are remarkably worthwhile.

Both Health Integration and the development of a constructive Self-Belief Identity are crucial to our wellness and well-being. Some people seem to grasp intuitively how to use these fundamentals. They take care of themselves physically, emotionally, mentally, and spiritually, and they foster strong, energizing relationships. They also see themselves realistically and affirmatively. Though they may not be aware of it, these people have predominantly Positive Core Beliefs.

However, at some point in our lives, almost every one of us will face terribly upsetting or devastating events. If we learn how to use the Health Integration essentials and continue to fortify our Positive Core Beliefs, we can come through practically any experience with a stronger Self-Belief Identity and greater Core-Related Health. The rest of this book focuses on how to become healthier, develop Positive Core Beliefs, and create a more dynamic sense of self. As noted earlier, Health Integration is one of the two fundamentals of Core-Related Health.

In the next chapter, we look at how our relationships play a vital role in the development of our Positive Core Beliefs and Self-Belief Identity. We will also explore how to expand our relational skills. In the following chapters, we will discuss how to improve the essentials of Health Integration and other Key Core Beliefs.

Please complete the Review Activity on the next page,
"HOW GOES YOUR HEART?"

REVIEW ACTIVITY
Chapter 2

Before going on to the next chapter, take a few minutes to better understand how you can achieve enhanced Health Integration. The following exercise illustrates how these five essentials contribute to our physical wellness and psychological well-being.

HOW GOES YOUR HEART?

In some cultures, the heart represents the whole individual—not just their emotions. Indeed, we could imagine that a person who was truly heartless would lack the core qualities of being human. It is easy to see the differences between someone who is disheartened or half-hearted and someone who is wholehearted.

People in one Central America community greet each other with the question, "How goes your heart?" Because our hearts characterize who we are, we can use this question to review our own sense of wellness and well-being. The five interrelated essentials of Health Integration are illustrated in the HEART diagram on the next page. Each one impacts the other four essentials. In order to achieve a high degree of integrated wellness and well-being, we need to understand all of them.

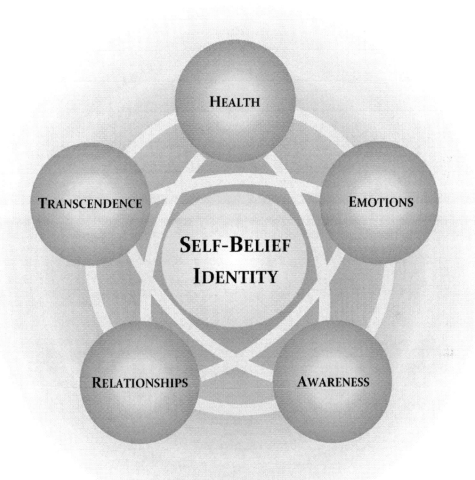

THE PERSONAL **HEART** REVIEW™

The Personal HEART Review answers important questions concerning your Health Integration. As you read each statement below, consider whether it accurately reflects how you have lived during the last six months. If the statement is completely true or almost completely true, place a check in that box.

To score the results of your Personal HEART Review, see page 30.

THE ESSENTIALS OF HEALTH INTEGRATION

HEALTH—developing physical wellness based on the principles of healthy living

- ❑   I enjoy healthful activities, such as walking, five or more days a week.
- ❑   I care for my eyesight, hearing, teeth, and my overall physical health, and I seek healthcare when it is needed.
- ❑   I do not harm myself with tobacco, alcohol, drugs, reckless driving, or dangerous activities.
- ❑   I sleep well for at least seven hours and feel refreshed when I wake up.
- ❑   I keep myself sufficiently hydrated, and I eat enjoyable, nutritious foods that include daily portions of fruits and vegetables.
- ❑   My weight is within a healthy range and I like the way my clothes feel on me.
- ❑   I live a simplified life without a lot of clutter and my home is well cared for.
- ❑   I enjoy living in my home because it is a wonderful place where I relax and renew.
- ❑   I appreciate the natural beauty of the outdoors and do not pollute my environment.
- ❑   I look for ways to improved my health and do what I can to stay healthy.

EMOTIONS—developing emotional balance and enjoyment
through self-understanding

- ❑ I consistently regulate my emotions when I am angry, sad, anxious, or resentful.
- ❑ I know how to soothe myself when I feel distressed.
- ❑ I handle stress well with humor, kindness, exercise, or other positive coping skills.
- ❑ I use a sense of guilt to change how I behave if I am incorrect or inappropriate.
- ❑ I realize shame beliefs (e.g., "I am bad," "I am ugly") are inaccurate and I strive to resolve any shame.
- ❑ I understand myself and regulate any impulsive behaviors.
- ❑ I am mindful of my feelings and I know how to appropriately express them.
- ❑ I recognize when I feel ACCUSED, GUILTY, REJECTED, UNLOVABLE, or POWERLESS.
- ❑ I foster becoming more WORTHY, ACCEPTABLE, and CAPABLE.
- ❑ I have a heartfelt sense of my worth and I believe, "I am worthy to be loved."

AWARENESS—developing the conscious use of our mental abilities

- ❑ I have a generally positive, realistic perception of myself.
- ❑ I feel a sense of appreciation, wonder, and enjoyment about my life.
- ❑ I continue to learn and improve through consistent personal development.
- ❑ I positively contribute to others and I am open to learning from others.
- ❑ I have five or more activities that I enjoy, and I regularly engage in fulfilling leisure interests.
- ❑ I do not compare myself with others.
- ❑ I believe mistakes are essential for my learning and growth.
- ❑ I evaluate my important life experiences to gain greater understanding and insight.
- ❑ I am clear about my values and rely on them to make effective decisions.
- ❑ I honor my promises to others and myself.

RELATIONSHIPS— developing caring and satisfying connections with others

- ❑   I am genuine—I strive to be consistently truthful, reliable, trustworthy, authentic, and sincere.

- ❑   I am respectful—I recognize that others have the right to make their own decisions even if I do not agree with them.

- ❑   I am empathetic—I listen and do my best to understand others and their emotions even when they are MAD, SAD, ANXIOUS, or distressed.

- ❑   I am accepting—I acknowledge others as they are, and I do not impose my expectations, values, or judgments on others.

- ❑   I am trustful—I recognize that most people are basically good-hearted, and I acknowledge the best about others.

- ❑   In each of my relationships, I create at least five positive interactions for every negative one.

- ❑   I ask others to forgive me and I make amends. I forgive others to free myself from resentments.

- ❑   I have close friends and/or a partner and do all I can to achieve our mutual best interests.

- ❑   I feel close to my family members, and I have worked through any past problems.

- ❑   I value the innate worth of every person.

TRANSCENDENCE—developing enrichment through inspiring and uplifting influences

- ❑   I value the diversity of life and enjoy natural beauty.

- ❑   I seek to be inspired and use uplifting influences for my personal guidance.

- ❑   I revitalize myself daily by reading positive literature or engaging in other enriching activities.

- ❑   I enjoy meditation, mindfulness, or prayer, and I am open to receiving inspiration.

- ❑   I nurture myself with encouraging thoughts, positive feelings, and constructive experiences.

- ❑   I consciously look for the blessings in my life.

- ❑   I practice thankfulness every day and frequently express my appreciation.

- ❑   I trust my intuitive instincts as a resource of valuable insight.

- ❑   I keep good thoughts in my heart for others and enjoy an abundance of love.

- ❑   I have a fulfilling life that is meaningful for me.

Scoring The Personal HEART Review™

Count the number of boxes you have checked for each of the five HEART essentials of Health Integration. Record your totals in the blocks below by coloring in the blocks in each column, starting from the bottom up.

Health	Emotions	Awareness	Relationships	Transcendence
10	10	10	10	10
9	9	9	9	9
8	8	8	8	8
7	7	7	7	7
6	6	6	6	6
5	5	5	5	5
4	4	4	4	4
3	3	3	3	3
2	2	2	2	2
1	1	1	1	1

When you have finished, take a few minutes to think about what you have learned. The Personal HEART Review can be used like a compass to chart increased Health Integration. It can help you visualize those areas that you may want to focus on. Give particular consideration to those areas you feel would be of greatest benefit to you. If you have any serious concerns, you may want to ask for assistance from a trusted friend or a healthcare professional.

We all know that ignorance limits our ability to respond to challenges and opportunities. Conversely, being more aware of positive qualities adds to our capabilities. One of the fascinating features of this review is that our added awareness makes us more subconsciously responsive to prospects for improvement. You can experiment with this by putting the review away for a while. Mark on your calendar a reminder to look at it again after three months. You will probably discover you have checked off more of the boxes and have achieved a greater degree of Health Integration.

Consider taking the Personal HEART Review regularly. Over time, as you become aware of the five essentials, it is likely your score will continue to naturally increase. To accelerate your progress, ask a trusted friend to serve as your adviser.

The adventure of life is like a canoe trip down a winding river. We do not know what lies around the next bend, what rapids might challenge us, the natural wonders we will see, or the people we will have the opportunity to meet. The journey of our life will be largely determined by how we respond to these new opportunities. The Personal HEART Review for Health Integration can increase our wellness, enjoyment of life, and fulfillment.

You can print out each Chapter Review Activity under the Activities tab at KeyCoreBeliefs.org. At the end of most of the Chapter Review Activities, you'll find a link to additional activities that are available without cost.

NOTES: Record any thoughts about Health Integration and the five HEART essentials: HEALTH, EMOTIONS, AWARENESS, RELATIONSHIPS, and TRANSCENDENCE.

CHAPTER 3

COMPELLING INTERACTIONS

How Relationships Shape
Our Core Beliefs

*When you talk, you are only repeating
what you already know.
But if you listen, you may learn something new.*

Dalai Lama

HOW CAN WE OVERCOME OUR
NEGATIVE INTERACTIONS WITH OTHERS?

Almost all of our Key Core Beliefs come into existence through our experiences with others. This started when we were babies, long before we began to form conscious memories. Contacts between infants and their parents or guardians have a huge impact on each child's development. Negative interactions do not always result in adverse consequences. However, the more positive connections a child has, the more likely he or she will develop Positive Core Beliefs and a constructive Self-Belief Identity. Naturally, the reverse is also true.

KEY CORE BELIEFS ARISE
OUT OF OUR EXPERIENCES WITH OTHERS

❑ For example, a teacher says to one student, "You are getting it." This reinforces a Positive Core Belief such as, "I am smart."

❑ The teacher tells another student, "You need to work a little harder." This might create a Negative Core Belief such as, "I am not smart, I am slow."

❑ Constructive interactions help us develop our Positive Core Beliefs.

❑ Unfavorable interactions contribute to creating Negative Core Beliefs.

❑ Many of the most important Key Core Beliefs that make up our Self-Belief Identity originate in childhood and adolescent relationships.

❑ The development of Key Core Beliefs continues throughout our lives.

Almost everyone will encounter highly distressing or traumatic experiences caused by other people. Regardless of when they occurred, none of these negative events have the power to permanently injure us. It is always possible to resolve these harmful, psychological experiences—and the Negative Core Beliefs that can result from them.

Studies of victims who experience a wide range of terrible events show that each of us is remarkably resilient and can recover from almost any prior condition. A particularly inspirational account is Viktor Frankl's story of his three-year imprisonment in a concentration camp during World War II. He describes his experiences in his book, "Man's Search for Meaning." By understanding his story, we learn how we can change the nature of our interactions with others and thereby improve the beliefs we have about ourselves. This amazing capability is available to each of us.

Unfortunately, many of us hold onto our past hurts and grudges. If we believe that we are forever victimized by past events, or if we are unwilling to resolve resentments with others, we can decline to work through how these events have hurt us. When we do this, we retain "the right to be a victim" or "the justification to be resentful." By rejecting the opportunity to address these issues, however, we also assume the responsibility for continually living with the resulting Negative Core Beliefs and the harm they create for our physical wellness and emotional well-being.

In our experience as mental health professionals, none of three authors of this book have ever encountered individuals who were better off feeling victimized or resentful. People do not become healthier or happier by refusing to resolve the hurts or injuries they suffered from the actions of others. Believe it or not, holding on to these hurts could be just as harmful as suffering injuries from a hit-and-run driver and then refusing to accept medical attention. And yet, many will not take care of their past psychological injuries.

One of the primary purposes of this book is to show how everyone can work through these issues, let go of these burdens, develop more Positive Core Beliefs, and live more enjoyable lives. Shelley's story is a good example.

SHELLEY'S STORY

Shelley is a person who was able to change her Negative Core Beliefs. When her mental health professional, Nori, met with her for the first time, it did not take long to find out something was deeply distressing her. "No matter what I do, I always make a mess of things for myself and everyone else," Shelley said.

To rephrase her statement into a Negative Core Belief, Shelley later said, "I am worthless!" As we have discussed, this kind of underlying belief can become pervasive. Through her interactions with others, Shelley's Core Beliefs adversely colored all of her perceptions and greatly degraded her sense of self-worth. For example, Shelley told Nori how she met her husband, Isaac. When they were introduced through a mutual friend, she said they felt an immediate connection and by their fourth date were already talking about marriage. Ten weeks after they met, Shelley and Isaac said, "I do."

But Shelly described her bitterness about never really getting to know Isaac before they married. She lamented that they had dated for less than four months. She felt disillusioned and almost betrayed when she discovered Isaac was not the man she had thought he was. The first few weeks of her marriage did not meet her expectations and then it went from "bad to worse." Now, some 14 years later with two children, Shelley felt trapped in a disaster of her own making.

A fascinating aspect of her story was Shelley's very strong belief that she deserved all the blame for their unhappy marriage. She thought she had blown her chances for a good marriage because she had not dated Isaac longer. Shelley had convinced herself that if only she had not rushed into the marriage, both of their lives would have turned out much better. She felt Isaac was a good guy but he should have married someone else. Now it was too late and there was too much "bad blood" between them. For Shelley, it was clear she had made a mess of her life, her husband's life, and the lives of their children. Although she was bitter with Isaac, she mostly criticized herself and believed she was responsible.

In addition to believing that she was worthless, Shelley had a number of other Negative Core Beliefs, including, "I am dumb," "I am helpless," and "I am a horrible wife and mother—I am horrible." As long as these beliefs persisted, Shelley assumed she was trapped in this dreadful situation. She had virtually no hope their marriage would ever improve.

It took about two months of concentrated effort with her counselor, Nori, for Shelly to replace her destructive beliefs with Positive Core Beliefs. She went through a process that included these four steps:

1. Become consciously aware of her Negative Core Beliefs (e.g., "I am dumb" and "I am horrible").

2. Convert these beliefs to more accurate and realistic Positive Core Beliefs ("I am capable" and "I am loving").

3. Take action to support the Positive Core Beliefs through constructive interactions (e.g., "Every day, I will find something good about Isaac and express my appreciation to him").

4. Continue to practice positive interactions (e.g., "I will establish a new habit of noticing at least five good things about others and then check-in with myself at the end of each day to see how well I did").

As she developed her Positive Core Beliefs, Shelley worked diligently with Nori to reprocess past, unresolved issues that had been traumatic for her. She confronted her negative thoughts and behaviors and learned how to skillfully regulate her emotions. In addition, Nori helped her develop the ability to forgive Isaac and others, and she increased her ability to empathize. Her efforts also strengthened a number of other Positive Core Beliefs such as, "I am kind and appreciative." All of these topics will be discussed in future chapters.

For Shelley, it was worth it. Within eight weeks, she began to see positive changes in her relationship with Isaac. Formerly spiteful arguments became manageable disagreements that led to workable solutions. She gained greater confidence in her ability to understand Isaac and to create options that worked for both of them.

For the first two months, Isaac was not interested in counseling. However, as he noticed how Shelley was more constructively interacting with him, he decided to join her. When they concluded counseling six weeks later, Shelley made an intriguing comment to Nori and Isaac. She said, "After the first two months of counseling, I had worked through so much that I no longer felt trapped. Even if Isaac had not joined in counseling, I would have continued my progress because my life and our marriage were so much more enjoyable. Instead of feeling stuck, I was free to create a new future." Shelley's Positive Core Beliefs changed how she experienced herself, her husband, and their marriage.

Her marriage started to take on new life. Shelley told Nori that she was giving herself permission to completely love her husband. More fundamentally, she began to value herself. She said, "I make mistakes. Everyone does. It's okay because I learn from them." She started to enjoy her children more and her friendships with others became more precious. Of course, Shelley and Isaac still had to deal with many of the same problems they had faced before. Now, however, they could work together as partners and their marriage became a wonderful friendship.

Shelley said, "Why would I ever go back? My life is so much better." Interestingly, she also noted an increase in her energy and overall sense of wellness. When she replaced her Negative Core Beliefs with Positive Core Beliefs, she improved her relationships, her mental and her emotional well-being, and she also boosted her overall Core-Related Health.

Shelley's story illustrates how our relationships shape our Key Core Beliefs. It also shows how these self-beliefs greatly influence our relationships.

PROCESSING OUR EXPERIENCES

Each experience we have is influenced by our Key Core Beliefs and the emotions related to those deeply held beliefs. As we perceive a new experience, our beliefs about ourselves directly filter and influence our perceptions. The diagram below illustrates this:

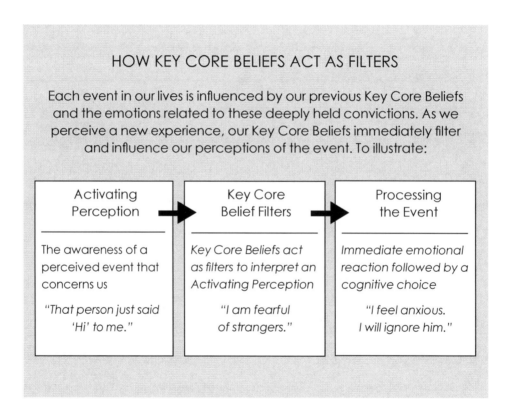

HOW KEY CORE BELIEFS ACT AS FILTERS

Each event in our lives is influenced by our previous Key Core Beliefs and the emotions related to these deeply held convictions. As we perceive a new experience, our Key Core Beliefs immediately filter and influence our perceptions of the event. To illustrate:

Activating Perception	Key Core Belief Filters	Processing the Event
The awareness of a perceived event that concerns us	*Key Core Beliefs act as filters to interpret an Activating Perception*	*Immediate emotional reaction followed by a cognitive choice*
"That person just said 'Hi' to me."	*"I am fearful of strangers."*	*"I feel anxious. I will ignore him."*

Our previous experiences combined with our Key Core Beliefs color our perceptions. For example, when Isaac criticized Shelley's shopping purchases, she filtered his comments in the context of their previous arguments about her spending habits. Shelley's Activating Perception was that Isaac was critical of how she spent money based on her own sense of somewhat erratic spending. If she believed, "I am untrustworthy," this Negative Core Belief would act as a filter to Isaac's comment. Therefore, she "Processed the Event" by deflecting her husband's criticism by accusing him of being a cheapskate.

If Shelley's Self-Belief Identity had been based primarily on Positive Core Beliefs, she would likely have talked with Isaac about how they spent their money. They then could have resolved the conflict in some way that worked for both of them. Individuals with strong Positive Core Beliefs rarely become defensive, because their perception filters are based on accurate Key Core Beliefs. When this is true, they almost always make an effort to develop mutually beneficial options.

Neuroscience has shown that our perceived experiences are emotionally processed within the limbic region of our brain moments before they are cognitively processed. In other words, we feel before we think. This emotional processing occurs in microseconds. Our limbic system interprets incoming sensory information so rapidly that it momentarily takes control before our ability to reason can come into play.

Our bodies are made this way because we have to be able to react very quickly to potentially threatening situations in order to employ the fight, flight, or freeze reactions. For example, when we are threatened by someone who is enraged, we do not have time to think about it. We simply react by defending ourselves or trying to get away—"fight or flight." Our Key Core Belief filters screen our perceptions in this emotional and cognitive processing.

In the previous example of an argument, Shelley's unconscious filters plus her semiconscious emotional reaction were already engaged before she cognitively processed what Isaac was saying to her. The stage was set for another quarrel about her spending, blaming accusations, and continuing reinforcement of her Negative Core Beliefs. Of course, all of these reflexive reactions were equally true for Isaac and his mental processing.

With each experience, our limbic system interprets our perceptions through the filters of our Negative or Positive Core Beliefs. In less than a second, our filters produce emotional effects followed by our cognitive reactions. Although it may not seem like it, every Activating Perception has some emotional context based on our Key Core Beliefs. Our beliefs greatly influence how we "Process the Event."

Gray, one of the authors of this book, explains how this happens by an experience with his sister that could have been interpreted in a number of different ways.

GRAY'S EXPERIENCE

I have an older sister who lives about an hour away. She usually comes for a visit about twice a month. If I see her unexpectedly drive up to our home, as an Activating Perception, I will have some kind of immediate emotional reaction before I use my cognitive reasoning ability. Since I have had a good relationship with her, it's likely that I will feel pleasantly surprised. My Positive Core Belief might be, "I am a caring brother." Therefore, I would Process the Event by warmly greeting her.

On the other hand, if our relationship has had a lot of tension, and she suddenly arrives at our home, I may be somewhat anxious. My Negative Core Belief might be, "My sister is unhappy with me, I am disappointing." In both of these contrasting situations, my Key Core Beliefs based on my prior experience with her would color my Activating Perception. The perception is the same; my sister is visiting. However, based on the filters of my Core Beliefs, my emotional interpretation of the perception could be quite different. In this situation, I might Process the Event by reacting coolly to her visit.

Let's consider a third example. Again, I see her drive up. We generally have a positive relationship, but in this situation, I start to feel badly because I recently said something unkind to her. My Negative Core Belief might be, "I am unkind" or "I am thoughtless." I could be anxious that she is going to scold me. I might Process the Event by becoming defensive, just waiting for her to say something negative.

Now, let's change the scenario a fourth time. In the past, my sister and I have had some really unpleasant interactions. Nevertheless, right now I am in a positive emotional state because I have just had a very enjoyable visit with my brother. This recent experience has stimulated my Positive Core Belief that "I am nice" or "I am caring." In this situation, I will more likely be able to deal with my sister's visit with less internal turmoil than I would if my Negative Core Beliefs dominated. In this situation, even if she were disagreeable, I could "Process the Event" by choosing to stay pleasant.

In all four examples, the event and the facts about the Activating Perception were the same (my sister arrived at my home unexpectedly), but my possible emotional reactions and Processing the Event would dramatically change. The filter of my Core Beliefs would significantly influence my cognitive ability to choose the way that I responded to my sister's visit.

These examples illustrate how our Key Core Beliefs filter our perceptions, impact our emotions, and influence our cognitive choices. Our self-beliefs most commonly alter our emotions without conscious awareness. In fact, even if we try to use our reasoning ability, chances are we will not be able to immediately change our emotional state. For instance, someone who has been previously snubbed by a friend and then unexpectedly runs into that friend in a store might try to act politely. However, any underlying resentment would continue to influence his or her emotions and interactions.

As noted, Gray's Key Core Beliefs acted as a filter and altered how he responded to the unexpected visit of his sister. The impact of Key Core Beliefs is part of this sequence:

- ❑   First, we perceive an event occurrence—Activating Perception.
- ❑   Second, we interpret our perceptions though the filter of our Key Core Beliefs.
- ❑   Third, our brain's emotional limbic system determines an immediate reaction that significantly influences how we choose to respond—Processing the Event.

No wonder many individuals feel trapped by their emotions! Think of someone who has held on to a grudge. It appears that the individual is powerless to change their feelings or their beliefs. Actually, this person could change, but mistakenly believes it is impossible to let go of his or her bitterness.

Escape the Trap of Feeling Powerless

When we believe, "I cannot change," this results in another Core Belief: "I am powerless." If we are convinced that we cannot do something, then it is absolutely true—we can't do it. It is likely that we will not even try. Therefore, we are helpless to change, even though that isn't true. But when we really believe we are helpless, this belief will override all evidence to the contrary. Our powerless self-belief becomes our truth. What might be feasible to accomplish literally becomes impossible for us. We are stuck—unless we first strive to transform our Negative Core Belief, "I am powerless," into a Positive Core Belief.

In contrast, the conversion of Negative Core Beliefs into Positive Core Beliefs not only has intangible benefits, it also has tangible ones. When an adult daughter challenged her dad to run a half marathon with her, he thought that it was the craziest idea he had ever heard. He was in his late 50s and had never run more than three miles. To run 13 miles was a nonstarter. However, when his daughter suggested he could run just a bit longer each day, he decided to take her up on her challenge. He changed his self-belief, began a training program, and ran a little further each time he went for a run. Not only did he complete this half marathon, he went on to run a number of full marathons.

The belief that we are powerless can also apply to our relationships. Some of the most famous stories in literature are about the grudges people have held towards others. You probably know of people who have not been able to resolve resentments, complaints, or other issues with family members or former friends. Sometimes people hang onto their resentments for a lifetime.

The story is told of two sisters who became professional rivals. After each had become offended by something the other had done, their bitter resentment lasted for decades. When the first sister died, still holding on to her animosity, the living sister was quoted as saying she was still unwilling to forgive. For over 40 years, both sisters felt completely incapable to resolve their differences and continued to embrace their mutual bitterness. Their resentment could not change until at least one of them decided it was possible to adopt a new way of believing. Neither did. They were both powerless because they continued to hold onto the poison of their resentments.

This is also true when we are unable to cope with our fears, anger, or depression. If we believe, "I am fearful," "I am bitter," or "I am depressed," we are trapped with these undesirable emotions and change is impossible. When this occurs, the additional Negative Core Belief, "I am helpless," creates a sense of complete powerlessness. However, if we begin to believe we can change, then new opportunities become possible and we can create more positive changes and more workable solutions.

It is not unusual for mental health professionals to work with individuals who do not respond positively to counseling. Some of them make limited improvement but then fall back to old patterns of thinking and behaving. They seem to be unable to make any real progress. Therapy may help with some of their symptoms, but it rarely addresses their underlying Negative Core Beliefs. Becoming discouraged, they give up hope of ever achieving a richer, more fulfilling life. On the other hand, when negative self-beliefs are replaced with Positive Core Beliefs, individuals frequently make life-affirming changes.

We know that anxiety greatly intensifies after a person experiences trauma or chronic distress. Once this anxiety develops, it creates triggers, or forceful reactions, associated with distressing events. These triggered reactions reinforce highly disruptive Negative Core Beliefs. It is these strong self-beliefs that become intrusive and often distort perceptions, feelings. and thoughts. They impede progress and block pathways to living better lives. However, even in these circumstances, Positive Core Beliefs can be developed to resolve the distress and alleviate the triggers. When this occurs, Activating Perceptions are changed through the filters of these Positive Core Beliefs and this results in more effective responses.

THE CAPABILITY OF THE FOCUSED MIND

Despite the intense emotional reactions that may arise out of unwanted self-beliefs, all of us have the ability to build constructive beliefs. When we do this, we create greater mental and emotional well-being as well as improved Health Integration. Each person has the capacity to learn new skills and then focus on applying these skills to transform Negative Core Beliefs. We can shift an undesirable belief (e.g., "I am poor at relationships") to a desired belief (e.g., "I can be more understanding of others") and, at the same time, reinforce another Positive Core Belief, "I am capable." This keeps hope alive even in the most difficult of interactions.

For example, people who become blind through injury or illness can adapt with remarkably enhanced abilities. Their brain quite literally changes to reflect the additional capacities of their other senses. By overcoming the loss of sight, many individuals develop new, more robust Positive Core Beliefs such as, "I am resourceful," "I am self-reliant," "I am highly competent," and "I am resilient!"

Can any of us imagine what it would be like to come out of a coma after an accident only to discover that we could no longer see? What thoughts would race through our minds? What beliefs would we form as we felt helpless and completely dependent on others?

Of course, many have had to contend with just such circumstances. As they adapted, their beliefs about being helpless started to change and they found they could do many things that initially seemed impossible. In these situations, MRI scans show how their brain activities are altered to become more aware of sounds and sensations of feeling. Their spatial sense also improves, and they increase their ability to accurately perceive their surroundings.

The same capability for dramatic transformation is true for all of us who strongly desire to modify the course of our lives, particularly in our relationships. Change becomes possible and probable if we understand the power we have to alter our Negative Core Beliefs. Our capacity to direct our minds through focused thinking and acting can help us overcome major difficulties and lead to much more satisfying interactions.

Whether recovering from addiction, conquering incapacitating panic, or overcoming debilitating health conditions, we can convert the stumbling blocks of our Negative Core Beliefs into stepping-stones that will shape a makeover of our lives. In almost every situation, relations with others will become increasingly satisfying.

Some individuals are more skilled than others in accomplishing these results. By studying what has worked for them, we can learn how they achieved interpersonal success, and then we can apply what they have discovered to develop better lives for ourselves.

How can we do this? Research confirms what many people already know. Regardless of a person's age, each of us has a tremendous capacity to continue to learn and to master new skills. If we want to join a sports team, develop a more fulfilling career, or play in a band—the road to success is the same:

We must practice!

How to change Core Beliefs from negative to positive

In order to change a Negative Core Belief, we first have to understand and identify the belief. The next step is to substitute an alternative Positive Core Belief. Below are a few examples of undesirable and desirable beliefs.

NEGATIVE CORE BELIEFS	POSITIVE CORE BELIEFS
I am ...	I am ...
boring	funny
sick	healthy
alone	friendly
hopeless	hopeful
depressed	optimistic
ungrateful	appreciative
angry	calm
critical	accepting
addicted	overcoming
ashamed	okay
lazy	conscientious
unlovable	worthy to be loved

Notice how all of the Positive Core Beliefs naturally support positive interactions with others. As we grow in our ability to interact more constructively, our Negative Core Beliefs can be transformed. We all do this when we change any aspect of our lives. For example, a young woman believed, "I could never be a costume designer. I am uncreative." However, she loved the theater and soon became engaged with others in every aspect of her high-school play. She focused on enhancing her creative abilities and reinforcing beliefs such as, "I like helping others—I am helpful" and "I am imaginative." She also took advantage of every opportunity to learn from others and to use her design skills. Later she remarked to her friend, "I never thought I was very creative but it turns out that I am. I also work well with others to come up with imaginative ideas. And guess what? I just got my first job as a designer."

Another person thought, "I am too old to go back to school; after all I am 47 years old and you can't teach an old dog new tricks." As long as she believed this, she would not even attempt to enroll in an educational program. However, after she saw a news article about a 63-year-old grandmother who just finished earning her high school diploma, she said to herself, "I could do that! I am always learning from others." The next day she made an appointment with a school counselor to see what programs were available, and soon she was enthusiastically working towards completing her educational dreams.

In these examples, both individuals became aware of their Negative Core Beliefs, "I am uncreative" and "I am too old to learn." They also realized how their interactions with others were instrumental in forming new Positive Core Beliefs. Next, they acted on their new, desired beliefs. Finally, they consistently practiced this Positive Core Belief. All of us have used this same process many times. It is how we learned to walk, ride a bike, add a column of numbers, drive a car, use a smart phone, etc.

But most of us were not fully conscious of how we changed our self-beliefs and learned to master a new skill. For example, in our early childhood, we did not know how to read. However, by believing that we could learn, we soon understood how to make sense of letters, words, and written thoughts. By contrast, those who have dyslexia may believe that they will never master the ability to read. Fortunately, we now better understand how to help everyone become proficient in reading.

We can become more mindful of the process needed to transform any Negative Core Belief. This process of change can be summarized in the following steps.

1. BECOME AWARE: Identify the Negative Core Belief
2. CREATE: Devise an alternative, desired Positive Core Belief
3. ACT: Foster behaviors that reinforce the Positive Core Belief
4. PRACTICE: Consistently act to strengthen the Positive Core Belief.

When we focus on applying this process, we become capable of developing richer, more fulfilling lives.

.

STRENGTHEN THE POSITIVE CORE BELIEF

Consistent practice results in our brain creating new neurological connections that strengthen our abilities. Developing any new skill is primarily a matter of practice or rehearsed exercise. In other words, what a person's mind focuses on and then repeats through intentional behavior will become more natural over time. The approach is the same whether we want to lift heavier weights, increase our understanding of a subject, or develop a better relationship. As noted in the previous sections, we first need to be aware of any Negative Core Belief, devise a preferred Positive Core Belief, act on that belief, and then concentrate on practicing behaviors that strengthen our new belief. As we focus and act on the belief, supporting interactions with others will greatly reinforce it. This is a method for achieving any desired result.

Concentrated practice is pretty straightforward and not difficult to do. In fact, visualizing a goal and then working to achieve it can be a lot of fun. Unfortunately, sometimes we give up too soon. We can achieve much more if we visualize practicing every day and if we use constructive interactions to strengthen our beliefs. This is especially true of transforming Negative Core Beliefs into Positive Core Beliefs. In fact, if we give up too soon, it may create another Negative Core Belief such as, "What did I expect? I am not persistent enough to achieve what I want."

To illustrate a positive example, one woman had a life-long dream to write a book about horses. Almost daily, she had to deal with a Negative Core Belief, "Who am I kidding? It takes a smarter person than me to write a book!" To overcome this belief, she had to first, become aware of it; second, change it to a Positive Core Belief ("I am capable"); and third, act in a way to support the Positive Core Belief. As she said, "I simply had to get back to my writing." She also asked a friend to help mentor her. Every day, that is what she did and the resulting book was a great success.

It may seem amazing, but we can restructure the connections in our brains through focused practice that reinforces Positive Core Beliefs. As we do this, the behavior becomes progressively easier until it becomes almost effortless. For instance, we changed our brains when we learned how to ride a bicycle or drive a car. In learning how to drive, at first everything seemed to be complicated and challenging. However, driving soon became routine and often required little conscious effort. For nearly everyone, there were others who encouraged us and helped us to master these skills.

How does this happen? Our brains constantly make new connections of neural networks that create additional capabilities. This capacity continues throughout our life, but it is up to us to develop it through our choices, our focused attention, and practice.

No one ever learned to drive a car alone or in one day. No matter what our circumstances, we choose to determine what we will mentally master. We will accomplish more as we engage with others through productive interactions and through sustained practice.

WE CAN SEE THINGS DIFFERENTLY THROUGH NEW POSITIVE CORE BELIEFS

At the beginning of this chapter, a diagram illustrates how our Key Core Beliefs act as filters. The example in the diagram illustrated an individual who reacted to her fears and avoided a stranger who had said "hi" to her. She later became aware of her Negative Core Belief. Then she created an alternative Positive Core Belief and took the necessary actions to reinforce this belief. With practice, she overcame her fear and learned how to be more outgoing in her interactions with other people.

The following chart summarizes how she accomplished this. This model can be used by anyone.

POSITIVE CORE BELIEF DEVELOPMENT

❑ BECOME AWARE: Identify the Negative Core Belief

   "I am scared around all strangers. My Core Belief is, 'I am fearful.'"

❑ CREATE: Devise an alternative, desired Positive Core Belief

   "I want to be self-confident. My Core Belief will be, 'I am confident.'"

❑ ACT: Foster behaviors that reinforce the Positive Core Belief

   "From now on, when someone greets me I will say, 'Hi.'"

❑ PRACTICE: Consistently act to strengthen the Positive Core Belief.

   "I will make a habit of this even if I feel anxious."

We all have the capacity to reprocess past experiences and thereby convert old Negative Core Beliefs into affirming Positive Core Beliefs. This increases our mental and emotional resiliency. However, reprocessing can only occur when we believe it is possible.

Through the development of Positive Core Beliefs, we can create richer, more satisfying relationships. Those people who have successfully worked on changing their beliefs commonly see themselves and others in a very different light than they once did. As they learn how to transform embedded undesirable beliefs, they experience their lives and their interactions with others in new ways.

As an example, one individual in her 40s said of her mother, "I got a new mom!" Of course, her mother had not changed, but the daughter's perception of her had become more positive because she had traded in her old, obsolete Negative Core Beliefs for Positive Core Beliefs. This changed how she perceived her mother and also how she saw herself.

Sandi, one of the coauthors of this book, experienced this change of perspective with her son when he was a senior in high school.

SANDI'S EXPERIENCE

If there is one constant I have learned that crosses over between my professional and personal life, it's that nothing escapes the effects of a Negative Core Belief! Therefore, I try to take my professional learning to heart for myself. This is also crucially important for me as I parent.

One day my son was trying to decide what he wanted to do after high school graduation. I encouraged him to take the time he needed, even if he decided to take a break from going on to college. As a mental health professional, I was thinking of all my teenage clients and the pressures they have because of the expectations their parents place on them. Therefore, I congratulated myself on being such an awesome mom who is so understanding!

It was then that my bubble burst. My son turned to me and said, "What? You don't think I can do it without taking a break?" Ugh. In his mind, he was struggling with a Negative Core Belief that told him, "I am incapable." My comment rubbed him the wrong way because it provided evidence to him that his mother shared this negative belief when that was not at all true.

Even with the best of intentions, I don't always get it right. No one does, and that's okay. I'm grateful that he said something to clue me in. Fortunately, because I know the power of Core Beliefs, I corrected myself and it turned out well for both of us.

His comment led to a further conversation about his future aspirations. Most of the time, I just listened. When he asked me what my thoughts were, I simply said, "Son, I think you can do anything you set your mind to!" I wasn't surprised when he decided to continue his education without a break.

We all make mistakes. Indeed, this is perhaps the most meaningful approach to learning and developing. Change is inevitable for each of us. But how do we make changes that reinforce Positive Core Beliefs through constructive interactions in order to create desirable outcomes?

NO MATTER, YOU CAN CHANGE NEGATIVE BELIEFS ABOUT YOURSELF
INTO POSITIVE ONES

Thousands of individuals have diligently worked to make their lives over into what they have always desired but never believed was possible. These include people who have:

- ❑ Suffered mental, emotional, physical, or sexual abuse
- ❑ Lived through severe trauma or chronic distress
- ❑ Been addicted to drugs, alcohol, gambling, pornography, or any other compulsive behaviors
- ❑ Been locked for years in seemingly hopeless marriages
- ❑ Experienced horrific combat trauma
- ❑ Had severe anger problems, sexual dysfunction, low self-esteem, depression, and anxiety concerns
- ❑ Been diagnosed with persistent mental disorders
- ❑ Survived traumatic criminal assaults

In fact, examples include so many varied problems it would be impossible to list them all. We can say with certainty—regardless of age, race, religious background, gender orientation, culture, or any other factor— Negative Core Beliefs can be transformed into Positive Core Beliefs.

Is this approach a cure-all for every problem? No—there is no magic pill, silver bullet, or easy answer. However, we can learn how our past undesirable interactions with others have been the basis for the unintended development of Negative Core Beliefs.

As Shelley's story at the beginning of this chapter shows, with better understanding and a commitment to practice supportive interactions, negative beliefs can be changed into Positive Core Beliefs. The benefits include:

❑   More enjoyable relationships

❑   Enhanced wellness and well-being—Health Integration

❑   The creation of more Positive Core Beliefs

❑   A strengthened Self-Belief Identity

❑   A greater sense of self-worth

The advantages of developing added Positive Core Beliefs through our interactions with others should not be underestimated. As we constructively interact with others, we strengthen favorable self-beliefs and our Self-Belief Identity. In addition, we also improve one of the five HEART essentials—RELATIONSHIPS. All of this comes together to expand the vitality of our Core-Related Health.

THE NEXT CHAPTER—TWO GROUPS OF INDIVIDUALS

In the following section, Transforming Negative Core Beliefs into Positive Core Beliefs, we will learn how distressful interactions can become resolved and how problematic relationships can be greatly improved. First, we will discover how all of us place ourselves into one of two groups. What are these two groups, and which one are you in? This is the subject of our next chapter, "Worthy of Love."

REVIEW ACTIVITY
Chapter 3

Please take a few minutes to explore the following questions:

How do your beliefs influence your emotions? Can you remember a time when you thought something was going to go badly only to discover that it turned out much better than you anticipated? What emotions did you feel before? How did you feel after?

When do you feel helpless, stuck, or powerless? (Gray Otis: I know I feel this way whenever my wife says the five most terrible words in the English language, "Gray, we need to talk." I also feel powerless when I'm stuck at a red light and I'm late to a meeting, when a friend does not understand me, when I cannot figure out something, and in countless other ways.)

What are the things in your life that you would like to change, but believe you cannot change?

Consider these questions for making desired changes to your life.

1. BECOME AWARE: What is my Negative Core Belief? Identify one of your
    Negative Core Beliefs.

2. CREATE: What is an alternative Positive Core Belief? Devise a desirable
    Positive Core Belief that would counter the Negative Core Belief.

3. ACT: What can I do to behave and interact with others in a way that reinforces the Positive Core Belief? What can I do to foster behaviors and interactions that reinforce the Positive Core Belief? Write down specific actions to support the desired new belief.

4. PRACTICE: Consistently act and interact with others to strengthen the Positive Core Belief. Daily evaluate what you have done to support your new Core Belief.

When we apply the process of developing Positive Core Beliefs, we become skilled at acquiring even more of these beliefs. Through practice and daily repetition, we reinforce corresponding constructive behaviors and interactions to achieve beneficial results.

This method for change has been proven to work. It does take time and effort, just like learning to skillfully drive a car takes patience learning how to drive and how to interact with other drivers. With consistent practice, we can achieve success and the results will be worth it.

You can print out each Chapter Review Activity under the Activities tab at KeyCoreBeliefs.org. At the end of most of the Chapter Review Activities, you'll find a link to additional activities that are available without cost.

NOTES: Use these pages to record any thoughts about the development of Positive Core Beliefs through constructive interactions with others.

Section Two

TRANSFORMING
ANY UNDESIRABLE
SELF-BELIEF

CHAPTER 4

WORTHY OF LOVE

The Most Crucial Key Core Belief

People will forget what you said,
people will forget what you did,
but people will never forget how you made them feel.

Maya Angelou

HOW CAN WE LEARN TO STRENGTHEN OUR KEY CORE BELIEFS?

What does my mirror really tell me? Bryson knew the answer to that question. He clearly saw that his mirror told him he was an example of "how not to live." Bryson truly believed, "Because of the way I have treated others, I am horrible." He also believed he was an angry person, a lousy father, a poor husband, and an idiot for never graduating from high school. Bryson was a hard worker, loved his partner and their children, and often helped others. Still, his Negative Core Beliefs intruded into every part of his life.

Bryson also realized there was one Negative Core Belief more significant than all of the others. It was the belief, "I am unworthy to be loved." After all, who could love someone who was "horrible"?

Indeed, we all could say one of two things about ourselves. Either

"I believe I am worthy to be loved!"

or

"I believe I am unworthy to be loved"!

Most of us never consciously consider if we deserve love. Even if asked, "Do you believe you are worthy to be loved?" most of us would immediately answer, "Of course I do."

But many of us who have substantial Negative Core Beliefs deeply believe we are undeserving to love or be loved. This is the most crucial Key Core Belief. It fundamentally impacts every aspect of how we live. It also critically influences all of our relationships. After all, how could anyone love someone who was actually unworthy to be loved?

WORTHY OR UNWORTHY TO BE LOVED?

The difference between "not worthy" and "unworthy" is important. To be "not worthy" implies a person at the moment—temporarily—lacks worthiness. For example, a father felt upset with himself because he lost his temper with his little boy. Because he felt guilty, he wanted to do better and this motivated him to go to his son and work things out. Soon, his sense of being worthy to be loved returned. His guilt prompted him to become a better father.

Those who deeply believe, "I am worthy to be loved," sometimes feel guilty but they seldom experience shame. Instead of believing, "I am a bad person," they would be much more likely to think, "I acted badly. I need to learn from this and act better the next time." This prompts them to be more aware of their emotions (in this case anger), regulate these emotions, and then act more favorably. Each of us makes mistakes. If we learn from them, we progress and have no reason to feel ashamed.

By contrast, if the father actually believed he was "unworthy to be loved," he would feel flawed. In addition to feeling guilt, he would also have experienced shame. He might have thoughts such as, "I am a lousy father. Why can't I stop losing my temper? My brother-in-law doesn't get upset like I do. There must be something wrong with me." Without being aware of it, he would believe, "I am unworthy to be loved."

Of course, the angry father is just one example of how someone might feel, but it illustrates one of the central characteristics of those who believe, "I am unworthy to be loved." If we have this belief, or any other self-belief based in shame, we assume something within us is fundamentally flawed. We are unacceptable, damaged, defective, or in some other way inherently inadequate.

THE POWER OF SHAME TO CREATE NEGATIVE CORE BELIEFS

Many of our worst self-beliefs begin with shameful experiences. These shame-based, Negative Core Beliefs often relate to a belief that we are unworthy to be loved. For example, if someone had made a series of mistakes, he or she might believe, "I am just awful!" or "I am a bad person!" If an individual had been abused or bullied, he or she may presume, "I deserved this!" or "I am such a weakling!" If a person had caused a serious accident, he or she might suppose, "What a fool I am!" or "I am irresponsible!" An infinite number of interactions can lead to labels of shame. And, in almost every case, there is also an unconscious belief, "I am unworthy to be loved." Who could love someone who is truly awful, horrible, deserving of abuse, weak, foolish, or irresponsible?

Shame-based Negative Core Beliefs are particularly potent—strong enough that they can produce depression and anxiety. If we continually believe we are ashamed, this creates constant unease regarding who we are. These feelings of shame are amplified by our misinterpretations of experiences that we mistakenly think confirm our Negative Core Beliefs. Quite frequently, shame experiences create a change in the sense of self, and this can lead to anxiety, depression, or other mental health problems.

Shame is defined separately from guilt. Guilt occurs when individuals believe they have acted contrary to their own values. This can be represented by any of the following statements:

"I did something wrong."

"I lied."

"I should have helped that person"

"I acted badly."

By contrast, shame indicates an inherent flaw in a person as illustrated by these statements:

"There is something wrong with me."

"I am a liar."

"I did not care enough to help that person—I am selfish."

"I am a bad person—I am bad."

Because shame-based, Negative Core Beliefs are often assumed to be inborn characteristics, we also believe we are incapable of changing them. For instance, if we have a temper, we may believe it is inherent—perhaps we were born with an angry personality. How could we change this if we have always been a person with a short fuse? Despite our best efforts to improve, the belief of innate inadequacy always lurks in the back of our minds. No matter what we do, we still have a temper and therefore it is impossible for us to really change. We are forever stuck with these Negative Core Beliefs.

This is totally untrue, yet because many of us believe our self-beliefs are accurate, we think a flawed part of us can never be altered, and so we eventually give up trying to change. We feel deeply trapped and lose all hope of ever becoming the person we really want to be.

DISTINGUISHING SHAME FROM GUILT

Negative Core Beliefs are often expressed with the words, "I am ..." such as, "I am uncoordinated." These "I am ..." beliefs are statements of "being" rather than "about behavior." If we say, "I am a bad person," this is a shame-based, undesirable belief about who we are. Shame suggests something is fundamentally wrong with us. It leaves us feeling ensnared because we think we cannot change who we are, even though nothing could be further from the truth.

On the other hand, if we say, "I acted badly," then we probably felt guilty for behaving badly. Guilt is an emotion that tells us we have done something—or failed to do something—that was ineffective, improper, or harmful. Guilt helps us reassess what we did and then change that behavior in the future. For instance, we might offer an apology, make amends if that is suitable, or work to change how we act in the future. In this context, guilt serves a very valuable purpose by empowering us to improve our feelings, thoughts, and behaviors when we have done something inappropriate. As we use guilt to make positive changes, we become more worthy, acceptable, and capable. We also reinforce these qualities as Positive Core Beliefs (e.g., "I am WORTHY, I am ACCEPTABLE, and I am CAPABLE"). These valuable "WAC" beliefs are discussed in Chapter 8.

To summarize, guilt is associated with how we act. By contrast, shame relates to who we believe we are. Shame is always related to Negative Core Beliefs, and the most fundamental Negative Core Belief is, "I am unworthy to be loved."

How shame-based Negative Core Beliefs develop

The process of forming Negative Core Beliefs is most commonly subconscious. However, this is how it might look if we could outline the development of shame-based Negative Core Beliefs, which confirm that we are fundamentally unworthy to be loved:

- ❏   I don't measure up because I always do dumb things.
- ❏   I am stupid.
- ❏   No matter what I do, I cannot change this because I was born this way.
- ❏   Obviously, something is inherently wrong with me.
- ❏   There is no hope that I will ever get better.
- ❏   No one could ever really love someone who is stupid like me.
- ❏   I am unworthy to be loved.

Most of us are not aware of how this happens. Nevertheless, you might be surprised to learn how many individuals can easily identify with almost all of the above statements.

Another way we can demonstrate how Negative Core Beliefs develop is with an example of two possible parenting responses to a young daughter, Susan, who just hit her little brother with a toy. One parent describes the girl's behavior by saying, "Susan, it is wrong for you to hit your brother." Susan would feel guilty and would be less likely to hit others in the future. Another parent might instead say, "Susan, don't hit your brother. You are a bad girl." If Susan's parents continue to label their daughter as bad, Susan might develop the shamed-based, Negative Core Belief, "I am a bad person."

The distinction between guilt and shame is crucial. It made a huge difference for Portia.

PORTIA'S STORY

Portia was the epitome of success. After finishing college, she met a man who became her best friend and husband and they had three lovely children. She felt fulfilled in a job that assisted people with disabilities. Well-respected in her community, she was also an avid runner and participated in several local charity races. Portia appeared to have it all together.

In fact, when she met her mental health professional, Carlos, her first words were, "I really don't know why I made an appointment to see you. Everybody, except my husband, Tony, would say, 'The last person who needs to see a shrink would be Portia.' I imagine this will be just a waste of time."

Portia seemed to have all the hallmarks of a wonderful life. Nonetheless, she felt something was wrong and she did not understand what it was. Although she did not know it at the time, she was stuck with a hidden Negative Core Belief. Portia deeply believed, "I am unworthy to be loved!"

As Carlos got to know Portia better, she told him she felt like an impostor despite her public successes. On the outside, she appeared to be the model of a caring mother, partner, and professional. On the inside, she kept wondering why all of her success never seemed to be enough. She said she was tired of trying to keep up the facade.

Oddly enough, one of her main Negative Core Beliefs related to growing up in a home with loving parents and one older sister, Helen. Unfortunately, her parents, teachers, friends, and others had often compared Portia to Helen, who was very successful in nearly everything. Portia was told that her sister was more athletic, smarter, less rambunctious, and more considerate. No matter what Portia did, she could never measure up to her sister.

We might think Portia should "grow up and get over it." However, from her perspective as a little girl, then as an adolescent, and later as an adult, she repeatedly got the message that there was something not right with her because Helen was so clearly superior. Portia had the same parents and environment as her sister, and therefore she should have been just as accomplished, smart, and kind. Although Portia excelled in many ways, she still constantly compared her shortcomings to Helen's successes and every time she did, she was "the loser." None of Portia's accomplishments could compensate for this Negative Core Belief. She believed her sister naturally deserved to be loved and she, Portia, did not. Though Portia never consciously thought she was unworthy to be loved, she later learned that this powerful Negative Core Belief was playing out in every aspect of her life.

Carlos helped Portia develop the most central Key Core Belief, "I am worthy of love." She learned that she deserved this love regardless of her accomplishments because love never needs to be earned. Once she recognized her faulty belief, Portia adopted the new belief, "I deserve to be loved no matter what!" Then her other Negative Core Beliefs also started to be transformed.

The circumstances of her life did not change, but after she quit comparing herself to her sister, she perceived her experiences in a different light and discovered a new inner peace. Essentially, how she saw herself changed; the mirror reflected back a new person. Portia confidently believed, "I am worthy to be loved, not for what I do but for who I am. I am enough."

You might not be surprised to learn that Bryson—who said at the beginning of this chapter, "I am horrible"—eventually expressed almost the same feelings as Portia after being able to feel worthy of love. Bryson wanted to do the right thing, but in his own eyes he thought, "I can never measure up." He, too, felt exhausted from trying to do what was expected of him.

To everyone but his family, he appeared to be a nice guy but inside, he lived with the daily devastation of "knowing" he was a failure. For example, he mistakenly thought that his angry outbursts towards his children proved to Bryson that he was a monster. Though he did not have Portia's accomplishments and did not make a lot of money as a construction worker, Bryson was a faithful and caring father who provided for his family and dearly loved his wife. Even in the midst of his own problems, he had always been a person who others could rely on. None of this mattered to him. As far as Bryson was concerned, he truly was a horrible person and obviously unworthy to be loved.

Portia and Bryson illustrate just two of many possible scenarios. Regardless of the circumstances, almost every person who is truly dissatisfied with their life carries a number of Negative Core Beliefs as well as the most unfavorable Key Core Belief, "I am unworthy to be loved." Any of us who are burdened with anxiety, depression, and other mental disorders experience this belief to some degree.

Whether we are aware of it or not, this particularly harmful self-belief overrides all other beliefs. It affects how we perceive our experiences. Therefore, it colors our thoughts, feelings, and actions, and impacts our relationships.

UNDERSTANDING THE WHOLE TRUTH

Both Bryson and Portia individually came to realize that this most central Negative Core Belief was totally untrue. Their mistaken beliefs had been based on partial truths and incorrect presumptions instead of the whole truth. It took real effort for each of them to understand their misbeliefs, resolve past experiences related to these false suppositions, and develop the means to fully believe that they were genuinely worthy to be loved.

Many of us have an incomplete understanding about who we are. We can be very critical of ourselves. As previously discussed, we often compare our worst qualities with the best qualities of others, and when we are asked to identify our strengths and shortcomings, many will identify more negative qualities than positive qualities. This is not coincidental. Our convictions about our deficiencies directly relate to specific Negative Core Beliefs. If our Negative Core Beliefs predominate, it is quite likely that we will also believe we are unworthy to love or be loved.

HOW WE CAN RECLAIM OUR SENSE THAT WE ARE WORTHY TO BE LOVED

Bryson's story has a positive conclusion that illustrates how we can develop the self-belief, "I am worthy to be loved."

BRYSON'S STORY

In therapy, Bryson learned that his early childhood experiences significantly contributed to a number of his Negative Core Beliefs. He remembered being bullied for two years when he was in middle school by a boy who was much larger than Bryson. During this time, he dreaded going to school. When he talked with his parents about what was happening, his father told him to settle the problem as a "man would."

Bryson's attempt to follow his father's advice resulted in a fight and a fractured arm. Bryson was so embarrassed, he told his parents his arm had been broken when he fell off his bike. Fortunately, a few months later, Bryson's family moved and the bullying stopped.

However, the beliefs he developed during this time continued to haunt him. These experiences formed the basis of his shame and his belief that he was unworthy of love. Later, his lack of a high school degree significantly reinforced other Negative Core Beliefs. In addition to believing he was weak, he also believed, "I am an uneducated chump." No evidence could convince Bryson that he was a skilled construction worker who could handle several different machines. When he got home from work, he drank to numb out his feelings of inadequacy. Often, he got angry with his wife and children. All of these experiences provided the proof of his shamed-based beliefs, "I am horrible," "I am hopeless," and "I am unworthy to be loved." When his wife left him, he felt there was nothing left to live for.

A good friend recommended that Bryson come with him to a group program for individuals with drinking problems. He followed his friend's advice. He also met an individual who helped him learn how he could resolve the past and create a truly worthwhile life. This person became like an older brother. Over the course of the next four months, Bryson's Negative Core Beliefs were transformed to accurately reflect who he is.

Now he says, "Sometimes I acted horribly but I have learned from these experiences. I'm not perfect but I am caring, I am dependable, and I am worthy to be loved! No matter what happens, I am never again going to let Negative Core Beliefs run my life." Bryson became a wonderful friend to his spouse and worked as a partner with her to lovingly raise their children.

A similar journey of self-discovery is available to us all. Regardless of our circumstances, every one of us is worthy to be loved. Was there ever a baby who should not have been given love and affection? No, of course not. Bryson knew this and so does everybody else. If this is true for others, it is obviously also true for each of us.

Nearly everyone formulates a number of Negative Core Beliefs. These combined beliefs often reinforce the most important Negative Core Belief, "I am unworthy to be loved." If not resolved, this belief leads us to perceive, feel, think, and act in adverse ways towards ourselves and others. Like Portia and Bryson, we may struggle for years and be unaware of these undesirable, shame-based beliefs. When this happens, we will misunderstand ourselves and our relationships in chronically problematic ways. We feel unsettled, dissatisfied, and unhappy.

We have discussed how Negative Core Beliefs contribute to many physical health problems. If we are suffering from a stress-related ailment, we should strive to resolve any unfavorable self-beliefs that might be linked to our physical concerns. In addition, most mental health symptoms will resolve when we work through our Negative Core Beliefs, particularly the belief that we are unworthy to be loved.

If we unconditionally believe we are love-worthy, we create a strong Self-Belief Identity. Typically, we have fewer doubts about ourselves and we continue to build constructive relationships. The quality of our relationships is essential to HEART Health Integration, and it enhances all of the other four essentials as well as our Core-Related Health. So much depends on one Key Core Belief, "I am worthy to be loved!"

As we will discuss in the next chapter, we can learn how to greatly strengthen this belief. It takes consistent effort but the rewards pay dividends of peace and fulfillment for the rest of our lives.

REVIEW ACTIVITY
Chapter 4

Consider how you handle feelings of guilt and feelings of shame:

Are you able to work through guilty feelings by changing how you think and act?

By contrast, do you ever feel stuck with shame because you think something is inherently wrong with you that you cannot change?

On a scale of 0 to 10 (10 being positive), how confident are you that you are completely worthy to be loved? What are the reasons you would assign this particular score?

10	
8	
6	
4	
2	
0	

Using the same scale, how self-accepting are you? People who are more accepting are less self-critical and judgmental. They are more likely to be at ease with themselves despite their awareness of personal shortcomings and some things they would like to improve.

10	
8	
6	
4	
2	
0	

Both of these scales are indications of a person's Self-Belief Identity. Individuals who feel they are really worthy to be loved generally score themselves higher on these scales. As illustrated in the next chapter, we all can learn how to strengthen our confidence that we are worthy to be loved.

You can print out each Chapter Review Activity under the Activities tab at KeyCoreBeliefs.org. At the end of most of the Chapter Review Activities, you'll find a link to additional activities that are available without cost.

NOTES: Use this page to record any perspectives you had as you read this chapter.

BLOCKING
THE HEART AND MIND

Understanding How We Cope

Challenges are what makes life interesting;
overcoming them is what makes life meaningful.

Joshua J. Marine

WHAT BLOCKS OUR WORTHINESS TO LOVE AND BE LOVED?

Unresolved distressing experiences interrupt our normal capacity to believe we are worthy to be loved. In the past, it was thought such experiences had to be traumatic to have a major impact on our self-beliefs. However, we now understand a wide variety of experiences can be so disturbing that they create Negative Core Beliefs. As noted previously, many of these Negative Core Beliefs are related to shame. These shame-based beliefs block our ability to believe we are worthy of love. Whether as a child or as an adult, trauma and chronically distressing experiences impair our ability to love and receive love from others.

How trauma and chronic distress affect our core beliefs

Psychological trauma occurs when people experience an event that is mentally and emotionally overwhelming. This can happen if a person's life is threatened or if danger of grave bodily harm exists, such as a car accident, criminal assault, or combat. We can also be traumatized if someone we greatly care about is threatened or harmed. In many of these cases, life after the trauma is severely disrupted, often leading to troubling memories, bewildering emotions, chaotic thinking, disrupted sleep, disturbing dreams, general anxiety, dysfunctional behaviors, or other conditions. By contrast, individuals who have resolved traumatic experiences no longer have these confusing feelings or thoughts and are able to move forward with their lives.

Chronic distress for children or teens can lead to developmental trauma or other conditions with associated unfavorable beliefs. Chronically distressful experiences may include emotional, physical, or sexual abuse, bullying, neglect, and many other upsetting conditions. These individuals may have the symptoms of general anxiety disorder (GAD), post-traumatic stress disorder (PTSD), or other stressor-related disorders. Experiencing trauma and chronic stress invariably results in a shift in Key Core Beliefs, and self-beliefs become more predominantly negative. Unless they are resolved, these problematic beliefs are carried into adulthood.

Trauma or anxiety disorders can develop at any point in a person's life. Some mental health treatment approaches have proven highly successful in resolving the underlying causes of these concerns by helping individuals transform Negative Core Beliefs into Positive Core Beliefs. This book was written so that individuals can learn effective ways to create constructive Key Core Beliefs. However, it is always wise to consider consulting with a mental health professional who specializes in trauma resolution when attempting to overcome the impact of emotionally overwhelming experiences.

Understanding chronically distressful and traumatic experiences

Most of us will encounter a traumatic event one or more times in our lives. In addition, almost everyone will contend with long-term distress. These situations can occur if we suffer from lengthy unemployment, if we are discriminated against, if we are consistently criticized, or if we experience other long-lasting, anxiety-provoking events. In many situations, the anxiety associated with trauma or chronic distress can also create depression. We can understand this more completely through the experiences of Jeremy. His story demonstrates how relatively small events can create Negative Core Beliefs.

JEREMY'S STORY

When Jeremy came in for his first visit with Katya, his mental health professional, he said, "I always feel depressed." Now in his mid-50s, Jeremy had a devoted partner who had been with him for more than 30 years. They shared a loving relationship with each other. He had a steady job and was successful at work. However, he felt his depression prevented him from achieving any true success. As Jeremy described his life, Katya was quite curious about his underlying Key Core Beliefs since he seemed to have so many aspects of a satisfying life.

After meeting with Jeremy a few more times, Katya noticed that his stories often related to his parents, particularly his relationship with his mother. Both of his parents had constantly worried about making ends meet, even though they both worked very hard According to Jeremy, his mother and father were very hard-working and did not seem to enjoy life very much. During his childhood years, it felt as though a gloomy cloud overshadowed his home life. His mother often told him, "If you don't expect much, you won't be disappointed," and she then related accounts from her own life that reinforced this belief. She told him how her mother had been upset about a number of the choices she had made.

For Jeremy, his mother's comments inadvertently created a pessimistic mindset that developed into Negative Core Beliefs. These beliefs shaped a distressing worldview that he carried with him every day. How had this happened? Jeremy had unconsciously misinterpreted his mother's statement. Instead of understanding what she had said, "If you don't expect much, you won't be disappointed," he mistakenly thought she meant, "I don't expect much, because you'll be a disappointment." This was not what she said, but Jeremy lived in fear that he would let down his mother. Seemingly unimportant events during his childhood and teenage years strengthened the Negative Core Belief, "I am disappointing." For instance, no matter how hard Jeremy worked to be a good student, he always believed his parents were unhappy that he had not done better.

Thirty years later, he was still unintentionally accumulating evidence that this Negative Core Belief was true. His belief was linked to another belief, "I am depressed and will always be depressed." Despite his many achievements, his professional success, his loving partner and children, and his friendly relationships with everyone, it was never enough. All of these positive affirmations did not change his Negative Core Beliefs. A perpetual cloud of discontent and frustration hung over his life. It was no wonder he believed he would always be depressed.

As Jeremy worked with Katya, he began to understand how he had misinterpreted the stories of his parents and misunderstood his own experiences. He was able to develop more accurate Positive Core Beliefs that were reinforced by past and current experiences. He conscientiously worked to develop these constructive beliefs. After seven weeks of consistent effort, Jeremy's chronic depression began to lift and he became more comfortable with himself. His confidence increased and his life became more enjoyable and satisfying. His belief, "I am disappointing," was replaced with, "I am enough!" He also believed, "I am worthy to be loved!"

Clearly, Jeremy's Negative Core Beliefs emanated from mistakenly interpreted childhood and adolescent experiences. These ideas had shaped an assumption that became another self-belief, "I am stuck." This had been "his truth" for many years.

Despite some difficult issues in childhood, there was no real trauma in his life. However, he had experienced "chronic distress" and this created a number of Negative Self-Beliefs, as well as a poor Self-Belief Identity. His accumulated child, adolescent, and adult experiences had adversely influenced him and became an underlying cause of his depression.

Note that the parents of any child who experienced chronic distress should not automatically be faulted. Many Negative Core Beliefs can be unconsciously transmitted from parents to children. Also, young children frequently misinterpret their experiences. Additionally, children may develop Negative Core Beliefs from experiences outside the home that parents are completely unaware of. And of course, it is important to note that every person is accountable for his or her own behaviors. Parents who loved their children and tried to do what they could should not be singled out for blame—not only because it's often undeserved—but because this never helps an adult to resolve childhood problems.

Chronic distress can occur at any point in an individual's life. For example, adults may develop increased self-doubts if they are suddenly thrust into a highly competitive work environment or their supervisors are very critical. If this persists, it would be unusual for them to not experience increased distress. Out of these experiences, some individuals will alter previously held effective Positive Core Beliefs such as, "I am competent," to increasingly Negative Core Beliefs like, "I must be an idiot."

We should note that not all depression or anxiety can be explained by Negative Core Beliefs. For example, depression symptoms may be due to medical conditions such as thyroid issues. Other factors, can create depression or anxiety symptoms that are usually transitory. Examples include a move to a new home, loss of a friendship, an injury or illness, an unexpected job termination, grief, etc.

However, mental disorders related to trauma or chronic distress usually have associated Negative Core Beliefs. If these Negative Core Beliefs are not addressed, the disorder rarely improves. Anyone who is dealing with significant trauma, chronic distress, anxiety or depression should consider seeking the help of a mental health professional.

In cases like Jeremy's, we've shown that even relatively minor stressors can produce Negative Core Beliefs. Adverse beliefs are created because we can't understand these experiences. Ironically, Negative Core Beliefs are often created to hypothetically make sense of these circumstances, but these beliefs are mistaken—they do not correctly explain apparently inexplicable events.

For instance, in many cases of abuse, victims try without success to explain what has happened to them. It is not uncommon for them to think, "I must have done something wrong. Maybe I deserved this" or "I should have stood up for myself." These inaccurate thoughts can morph into shame-based, Negative Core Beliefs such as, "I am broken" or "I am weak" or "No one could ever love me. I am unlovable." For many individuals, these beliefs will affect how they interpret their future experiences. Unless these beliefs are resolved, they will create added misinterpreted experiences and other incorrect convictions.

Understanding Negative Core Beliefs and their tremendous influence over us is crucial to dealing with our personal problems as well as the difficulties they cause for our relationships.

How Negative Core Beliefs affect relationships

We have discussed in previous chapters how Key Core Beliefs constructively or destructively impact the quality of our interactions with loved ones and others. Unnecessary divorces often reflect underlying Negative Core Beliefs originating in the childhood experiences of one or both partners. Usually neither partner is aware of how these beliefs work just below the surface of their struggles. If harmful beliefs are not resolved, conflicts continue unabated, couples become estranged, and families fall apart. This is tragic because of all the unnecessary pain, and because many people never really understand what happened. Therefore, similar issues can occur again in the relationships that follow a break-up.

As tough as it can be for adults to identify how their own Negative Core Beliefs impact their relationships, it is also true that many of us fail to understand that so-called "problem children" have frequently experienced trauma, developmental trauma, or chronic distress. Many parents, teachers, and mental health professionals do not actually comprehend what prompts children to behave inappropriately.

Young people who act out are often undesirably characterized and labeled. A so-called solution to these misbehaviors is to discipline these children in order to make them compliant. Obviously, compliance with norms is often necessary, but imposing unrealistic expectations on children without really understanding them simply adds more Negative Core Beliefs to the other beliefs they already have—and usually doesn't improve the behavior. Even marginally adverse behaviors may have their origin in repeated distressful experiences. Rather than label children, we need to redouble our efforts to understand the underlying beliefs that prompt their behaviors.

Although related to a lack of self-esteem, that lack doesn't fully explain Negative Core Beliefs. Neither children nor adults can simply be reinforced with positive affirmations and then be expected to develop an enhanced Self-Belief Identity. As was the case with Jeremy, whose story appears earlier in this chapter, constructive confirmations, accomplishments, and compliments are ineffective in changing deeply ingrained Negative Core Beliefs. Though positive validation can be supportive, it is never enough to transform what we believe about ourselves. Instead, as illustrated in the next chapters, all of us can learn how to transform Negative Core Beliefs in order to develop a strong, internal sense of self-worth.

THE MIND CAN CHANGE THE BRAIN

Neuroscience has advanced a great deal in the last few years alone, but while we now better understand how our brains function, we still don't know how the mind alters the brain in creating new neurological connections. However, evidence shows that we all have tremendous capabilities to change the function of our brains through awareness and modified mental processing. As we understand Negative and Positive Core Beliefs, we can learn how to generate new, more beneficial belief systems.

HARRISON'S STORY

Harrison, a combat veteran, was diagnosed with severe PTSD related to an explosion that killed many of the soldiers in his unit. He suffered from severe headaches, consistent nightmares, periodic panic attacks, and frequent outbursts of rage. Lee, his mental health professional, explored the resulting Negative Core Beliefs and Harrison's related high level of distress. It is easy to understand why Harrison rated his level of distress concerning this horrific combat experience as "10" on a scale of 0 to 10. What's not so easy to understand is that his primary negative belief was, "I am gutless."

As Lee met with Harrison, he asked if Harrison had had any other experiences that were also highly disturbing. Immediately, Harrison referred to a very upsetting situation in his childhood. The level of distress he felt regarding this experience was also a "10." Harrison was able to identify an associated Negative Core Belief, "I am weak." For the next two weeks, this belief became the initial focus of counseling. After it was successfully replaced with Harrison's chosen Positive Core Belief, "I am resilient," Lee planned to refocus treatment on the combat trauma.

At this point, however, Harrison told Lee that his PTSD symptoms had subsided to such a degree that they were no longer significant. His headaches were alleviated, his nightmares had disappeared, he no longer had any panic attacks, and his anger was greatly reduced. In addition, he was no longer plagued by his previous Negative Core Belief, "I am gutless." He now believed, "I am effective." Subsequent sessions over the following two months validated the effectiveness of this approach, which had resolved both the childhood and combat experiences. There was no reported recurrence of any of his PTSD symptoms.

Harrison's situation illustrates the value of transforming Negative Core Beliefs. Successful ripple effects typically occur once these beliefs are understood and resolved. While not a panacea, effectively creating Positive Core Beliefs also transforms other troublesome thought patterns, producing a number of desirable results, including:

❑ Effectively dealing with the origins of mental and emotional concerns

❑ Lasting positive outcomes

❑ Improved relationships

❑ Increased appreciation and enjoyment

❑ An added sense of meaningful purpose

❑ Enhanced physical wellness

❑ Increased emotional resilience and well-being

❑ A strengthened Self-Belief Identity

These outcomes are indications that Negative Core Beliefs have been converted to Positive Core Beliefs. All of the authors of this book have observed many people who developed these encouraging beliefs and achieved all of the outcomes listed above. We also have experienced these transformations ourselves.

These transformative changes illustrate that changing our minds through the development of Positive Core Beliefs effectively influences the brain. Previous traumatic triggers continue to diminish until they are not a concern. Anxiety is reduced and depression is often alleviated so that these conditions are no longer problematic. Our mind's capacity to help restore our brain's functioning is quite remarkable.

Key Core Belief development

As we become aware of Negative Core Beliefs, we can replace them. When we do this, we become more mentally and emotionally resilient. Sometimes we will need the help of a mental health professional. In many situations, however, we can learn on our own to become conscious of undesirable beliefs and then act to create constructive beliefs.

The two separate accounts of Sabrina and Dale further illustrate the process of developing Positive Core Beliefs.

THE STORIES OF
SABRINA AND DALE

In her late teens, Sabrina was raped. After the attack, she understandably felt very vulnerable and unsafe. She turned inward, gave up most of her social relationships, and did not leave her home unless absolutely necessary. Sabrina's experience indicates some of the possible symptoms of post-traumatic stress disorder (PTSD). Increasingly, she turned to strenuous physical exercise for two hours every day as her primary coping mechanism. She developed new Negative Core Beliefs such as, "I am unsafe, I am untrusting, I am a loser (for putting myself in that situation), and I am damaged."

Dale, at age 7, had to repeat first grade because of poor language and math skills. He was embarrassed and ashamed to be held back. His experience was aggravated by a younger brother who was exceptionally bright and learned to read and write at a very early age. Dale responded by becoming belligerent and isolating himself from others. As a young adult, he had just two friends, rarely left his apartment, played a lot of video games, and had recurrent bouts of depression and anxiety that were treated with prescription medications. Dale's beliefs included, "I am a failure, I am dumb, I am a burden, and I am incapable of doing anything right."

Though Sabrina's and Dale's circumstances differed greatly, both of their experiences resulted in changed perceptions of others and changed beliefs about themselves. Sabrina and Dale both became certain that they were unworthy of love. Each of them had been trapped by harmful self-beliefs as well as highly ineffective coping mechanisms.

Certainly, what Dale experienced is in no way comparable to Sabrina's horrific sexual assault. However, these very contrasting stories illustrate how the development of Negative Core Beliefs can result from extremely horrific experiences as well as much less serious events.

Dale's experience does not mean that children should never have to repeat a grade. Nor does Sabrina's sexual assault indicate that everyone who has been brutally attacked believes it was his or her fault. Rather, it's clear that what is especially disturbing to one person may not have the same impact on another.

For instance, some soldiers who faced very distressing combat experiences seem to be able to work through them much more effectively than others. However, research has shown that repeated exposure to traumatic events significantly increases the likelihood of developing anxiety. Accumulated distress eventually takes its toll on everyone.

Interestingly, an experience that may have little or no effect on a person at one point may at other times be highly disturbing. For example, individuals may initially recover from the overwhelming emotions of a life-threatening automobile accident. Yet years later they might suffer significant anxiety from a minor accident during a snowstorm. There are so many variables that the impact of our emotional experiences at different times cannot be predicted.

Fortunately, Sabrina and Dale both received the help they needed. Dale learned about his Negative Core Beliefs and worked diligently to resolve them. During this time, he discovered that he had an uncommon talent for diagnosing electronic problems. After completing a challenging technology course, he became a highly successful technician. Although he was naturally comfortable living alone, he found work associates and others who understood him. Eventually, he came to enjoy an expanded circle of friends. As he became more self-assured, he said, "I am pretty smart in so many areas. I am also very caring of others. But, regardless of this, I know I am always worthy to be loved."

Sabrina sought out a mental health professional who specialized in treating trauma. They worked on resolving the rape experience as well as the resulting Negative Core Beliefs, "I am damaged. Nobody could ever love me. I am broken." After about three months, Sabrina's efforts paid off and she achieved greater self-awareness. Her new Positive Core Belief became, "Of course, I am lovable! Anyone who has gone through what I have and bounced back is a strong person. I am resilient and I am also compassionate."

Sabrina and Dale never met each other, but if they had discussed their different experiences, they would have recognized a few important similarities. The most significant similarity would have been their Negative Core Belief, "I am unworthy to be loved." Among their other beliefs, this one was the most crucial.

UNDERSTANDING HOW TO DEAL WITH TRAUMA AND CHRONIC DISTRESS

The complexity of each person's psychological mind and physiological brain can be compared to the vastness of the universe. We may never fully understand how these extremely intricate mental functions work. Every person's mind and brain are constantly developing.

The accumulation of our experiences is totally unique to us. No one can actually "walk in another's moccasins," go through what they have gone through, or feel what they have felt. It may be well-meant for one person to say to another, "I really understand what you're feeling" when both people have had the same experience. Keep in mind, however, that they each have had their own interpretations of that experience. It is impossible to completely comprehend another's feelings. Sometimes, it is difficult enough to understand our own. Even those in the helping professions, such as physicians and mental health professionals, can never presume to know the internal experiences of another person.

Countless different circumstances can result in a wide variety of Negative Core Beliefs. These powerful beliefs often block our ability to get over distressing experiences in order to move our lives forward. When we feel stuck, we also frequently feel something is fundamentally wrong with us.

Trauma and chronic distress frequently result in future experiences that seem innocuous to others but that trigger strong reactions. For example, a person who has been constantly criticized by a spouse may feel extremely belittled if a friend suggests he or she should not be "so uptight." These intense emotional reactions produce a degree of impairment that can become persistently problematic.

Trigger experiences may occur repeatedly over a period of time and may be persistent. Regardless, individuals who suffer from the effects of traumatic or chronically distressful experiences often develop highly charged Negative Core Beliefs. These adverse beliefs continually diminish the quality of their lives.

Some believe there is no way to change our past behaviors and beliefs. However, this isn't true; we can learn effective means to overcome almost every mental health concern. Ty's story illustrates how feeling hopeless can be transformed into personal and interpersonal success.

TY'S STORY

For years Ty was convinced, "I am an angry person." He was certain he had always been angry and always would be angry. It was as if he thought he had been born with an "anger gene." Therefore, there was no point in trying to overcome his problem. He had tried and failed many times.

Ty felt stuck with this Negative Core Belief. Despite many efforts to change, no matter what he did, he still had a lot of resentment, anger, and rage. He was ashamed. Notwithstanding a strong value to control his temper, he could not stop feeling upset in many, many situations. It did not take much for him to explode, and this almost always occurred at home, with his anger directed at his partner or one of his children. They experienced the full force of his rage. Once, he became so enraged that he slammed his fist through a wall. His anger was so bad that he could have been charged with domestic violence. He knew his wife and children couldn't trust him.

Ty's Negative Core Belief, "I am angry," was untrue. However, it was the only "truth" he believed. He was also convinced, "I am unworthy to be loved." He put it this way, "Everybody except my family thinks I am a really nice guy. If others knew I was really a raging maniac at home, they would be shocked. I am such a hypocrite and I can't do anything about it."

His bitter anger continued for more than 20 years. Finally, a friend recommended, Kia, a mental health professional. After meeting her, Ty readily agreed to work with her, and over the course of three months, he made a consistent effort to change his Negative Core Beliefs. Daily, he practiced how to exchange his previous self-beliefs with Positive Core Beliefs. He conscientiously tried to better understand his emotions, he resolved the chronic distress of being criticized as a child and teenager, and he overcame his conviction that he was unworthy to be loved. In addition, he began to visualize new ways to calm himself and interact positively when he recognized he was becoming annoyed, irritated, or resentful.

After seven weekly counseling sessions, he began to see real changes in his ability to work through emotionally challenging events. Naturally, it took more weeks of practice to solidify these changes. It also took several months for his wife and family to trust that he had really changed for good.

Ty was amazed by his ability to regulate his anger and eliminate it as a source of contention in his family. The results were profound for him, his wife, and his children. At one point, he actually said to his mental health therapist, "You know, I really am worthy to be loved. I always have been but I never believed it." A few years later, Ty went back to school and became a mental health professional because he wanted to help others with severe anger problems.

People who deal with anger and rage frequently feel powerless because of circumstances they have no control over. When this happens, they become more impatient, their lives become more chaotic, and their anxiety increases. Their anxiousness may be almost unnoticeable at first, but their feelings nearly always become more disturbing and unmanageable. Many individuals do not express anger at work because it would be too embarrassing. Instead, they become irritated and outraged with family members. Little frustrations turn into criticisms, resentments, and then outright fury. After exploding, they often feel contrite and want to make amends.

However, the cycle of anger invariably creates emotional abuse and often physical abuse. Rage behaviors can result in domestic violence. Even chronic resentment terribly impacts the lives of many families. In addition, all forms of anger continue to fuel Negative Core Beliefs. If these underlying beliefs are not resolved, the offender is blocked from recovery and the cycle is repeated, again and again.

WE CAN BE HEALED

Each of us can choose to overcome our shame and any related Negative Core Beliefs. This path of progress is available to everyone. Some will be able to use the tools in this book to transform detrimental beliefs into Positive Core Beliefs. Others will need the help of a trusted friend, minister, family member, or mental health professional to assist them. Regardless of the circumstances, the goal is to believe, "I am worthy to be loved."

In working with his counselor, Ty identified four of his Negative Core Beliefs:

❑   "I am weak."
❑   "I am undependable."
❑   "I am powerless."
❑   "I am judgmental."

Once Ty became aware of these beliefs, he worked with Kia to understand when he became triggered. He then devised alternative Positive Core Beliefs and acted to create effective outcomes. For example, when he arrived home to find his daughter's bike blocking the middle of the driveway, he learned to realize that he was feeling powerless. His alternative belief was, "I am capable!" He then acted on his awareness and his new positive belief. He took a deep breath, went inside the house to find his daughter, and asked her to put her bike in the garage. Much to his surprise, she did.

The bike-in-the-driveway situation happened many times. However, rather than give into his anger, Ty recognized the crucial importance of practicing what he had learned. He used soothing self-care and positive interactions to achieve improved results. As he acted in a more encouraging way, he felt much better about how he was handling these kinds of circumstances. Slowly, he began to trust that he was a genuinely caring dad. Just as importantly, his daughter started to trust that he would not explode with rage. This worked so well for Ty that he could not imagine going back to his old angry behaviors. Over time, his daily practice that changed his beliefs, combined with more constructive interactions and consistent practice, created new neurological connections.

Negative Core Beliefs lie at the root of so many of our problems and yet we so often are not consciously aware of them. After bringing them to our awareness, we can devise alternative Positive Core Beliefs, act on these beliefs, and practice them. This becomes a much more successful way of dealing with anxiety, depression, anger, and other concerns rather than relying on ineffective coping mechanisms.

Harmful coping mechanisms

Negative Core Beliefs, which foster undesirable cognitive patterns, often lead to psychological as well as physiological symptoms. Most people know that excessive anxiety may cause ulcers. It is also true that chronically distressing, Negative Core Beliefs can bring about a great variety of other physical health problems and mental concerns.

For example, people often turn to detrimental coping mechanisms such as drug or alcohol use, as well as other compulsive behaviors, to counter their Negative Core Beliefs. Many of us have little or no awareness of these self-beliefs, but our dysfunctional coping behaviors are easy to identify. Therefore, if our lives start to go off the rails, we typically focus on the obvious behavioral problems (drinking, drug abuse, self-harm, gambling, etc.) rather than the underlying cause of the behaviors. Mental health professionals who work in the field of addiction recovery know that those with compulsive behaviors also have a number of self-destructive beliefs. Their harmful convictions significantly contributed to the origin of their compulsions and often dominate every facet of their lives. True recovery from addiction or any detrimental coping behavior requires the resolution of these Negative Core Beliefs.

Shame-based Negative Core Beliefs are so emotionally uncomfortable that we will do almost anything to avoid the discomfort. The thoughts and behaviors we use to avoid feeling these emotions are called coping mechanisms. For example, people who believe, "I am stupid," may feel very distressed if asked to give a speech or to perform. They might try to escape speaking by excusing themselves. Making an excuse uses the coping mechanism of avoidance.

Many coping mechanisms are maladaptive. Not only do they cause problems in and of themselves, very frequently, they strengthen multiple Negative Core Beliefs. In the previous example, individuals who always find an excuse to avoid speaking might say to themselves, "Nobody wants to hear what I have to say." "I would just make a fool of myself." "I am an idiot for thinking anyone really cares." In other words, "I am stupid" and "Who would love someone stupid like me!"

THE TRAPS OF HARMFUL COPING MECHANISMS

The number of maladaptive coping mechanisms is infinite. When a coping mechanism is used repetitively, it can become a compulsive pattern of behavior. A few examples include:

❑ Explosive anger or getting into arguments or fights
❑ Working too much
❑ The abuse of alcohol, drugs, or medications
❑ Thinking simplistically, such as black-or-white thinking

❑   Repetitive dishonesty and lying
❑   Problematic eating patterns
❑   Pornography
❑   Dangerous, risk-taking activities
❑   Excessive exercising
❑   Self-harm
❑   Problematic use of avoidance
❑   Too much video-gaming
❑   Excessive spending
❑   Depending too much on others
❑   Addictive gambling
❑   Watching too much sports or TV
❑   Engaging in any compulsive behavior

We turn to these and many other harmful coping mechanisms for temporary relief. However, they can often become traps. In many situations, the repetitive coping behavior becomes a compulsion that cannot be stopped. Also, negative means of coping almost always create other troubling concerns. For instance, excessively exercising can lead to health issues such as stress fractures or malnutrition.

Many mental health disorders and the resulting dysfunctional behaviors could be described as ineffective means of coping. Most problematic coping mechanisms are commonly created without our conscious awareness that we are trying to deal with the distress of underlying Negative Core Beliefs. In addition, adverse coping mechanisms divert our attention away from the undesirable self-beliefs that lie at the root of our problems.

For Ty, his coping mechanism was enraged fury. Stress would build up until his anger exploded at his children or his partner. Afterwards, he always felt ashamed. He wanted to do better. While his stress temporarily subsided, the pattern would be repeated. Sooner or later his stress would increase until he reached the point of exploding again.

Sabrina and Dale adopted other adverse coping mechanisms. For instance, they tried to avoid situations where they would feel unsafe and therefore they never went anywhere that was unfamiliar. This is a mental health disorder known as agoraphobia, a condition where an individual becomes anxious when they leave the safety of their home or familiar surroundings. When they go outside, they believe they have little control over what might happen. They may feel truly safe only at home. Sabrina and Dale rarely went out unless they had to. The idea of going to a new place was so stressful that it was much easier to just stay home— where they were in control.

But this was a trap. Both Sabrina and Dale knew their fear of going out was irrational. But they also knew they were helpless to change their unsafe feelings. Because of this unreasonable state of mind, they became stuck inside and caught in their own unreasonable fears. Sabrina said, "Who could love someone who cannot even overcome the totally irrational fear of leaving the house?" With this negative belief, it is understandable why Sabrina was unmarried. Dale had been married for five years but never wanted to go out with his wife or child. Both Dale and Sabrina were strongly convinced they were irreparably damaged. Their coping mechanism did not work; they felt powerless to change and trapped in their own fears.

When Negative Core Beliefs combine with fear, harmful coping mechanisms are often created and individuals invariably conclude, "There must be something wrong with me." Because we feel helpless to change, we also think we are unworthy to be loved. Whether we blame ourselves or others for our problems, our lives feel uncomfortable and our relationships suffer. It seems that escape is impossible.

All harmful coping mechanisms produce mental and emotional blocks that lead to the development of additional Negative Core Beliefs. We can get rid of harmful coping mechanisms and our Negative Core Beliefs. But we can't do this until we recognize the self-beliefs underlying our problems, transform them into Positive Core Beliefs, and then affirmatively act to consistently reinforce these new beliefs through constructive interactions.

CONSTRUCTIVE COPING SKILLS

We *can* develop means of coping that are helpful. All of us feel stressed, anxious, angry, or sad at times. If we learn how to positively deal with these emotions, we will develop skills that will enable us to effectively regulate our stressful emotions. We refer to these as coping skills because they enable us to work through troubling emotions in productive ways.

For instance, many individuals are highly uncomfortable with public speaking. One effective coping skill would be to practice deep breathing for a few minutes. Breathing deeply has been shown to help people feel less anxious because it provides added oxygen to the brain and often reduces our nervousness. Many individuals use this coping skill to manage distress or anxiety. Other coping skills are reviewed in later chapters of this book.

NOTHING IS FUNDAMENTALLY WRONG WITH ANY OF US

Individuals with mental health concerns almost always fear something is fundamentally wrong with them. For Ty, it was his uncontrollable anger and believing that he was inherently an angry person. For Sabrina, it was the belief that she was unsafe. For Dale, it was the conviction that he was stupid. Ty, Sabrina, and Dale believed they did not deserve to be loved because they actually thought that they were deeply flawed. Their harmful coping mechanisms further convinced them of their unworthiness to be loved.

All detrimental coping mechanisms confirm our worst beliefs about ourselves. We think we are helpless and that no matter what we try to do to stop these behaviors, we are destined to go back repeatedly to the same ways of coping. Our embedded Negative Core Beliefs prevent any real recovery, leaving us feeling ashamed and believing falsely that nothing will break this endless cycle.

Of course, at times, we positively interact with others, so our shame is suppressed for a while. When this happens, we imagine our life is going to get better. Unfortunately, this hope is almost always an illusion because we have not resolved the underlying Negative Core Beliefs. Our lives do not improve and soon the cycle of harmful coping resumes, thus reinforcing the fundamentally false belief of our flawed nature.

Even if a self-belief is totally false, when we believe it to be true, the belief has power. What we believe about ourselves is our reality. All of our Negative Core Beliefs have tremendous power to convince us that they are factual. If we believe, "This is the hand of cards that life has dealt me and there is nothing I can do about it," then we become convinced that we are hopelessly trapped. In addition, we often assume that we can't change our harmful coping mechanisms. Few things are worse than feeling stuck with these beliefs along with unwanted coping mechanisms.

However, we do not have to remain stuck with any false self-beliefs. Even when a self-belief is reinforced by actions, such as compulsive lying, the conviction, "I am a liar" can be changed to, "I am honest." In fact, there is no Negative Core Belief that cannot be transformed into a Positive Core Belief.

RESOURCES FOR RESOLVING NEGATIVE CORE BELIEFS

Each of us can work through our Negative Core Beliefs. Not only can we be free of the entangling snares of our shame-based beliefs, we can also be free of all harmful coping mechanisms. Sometimes that happens when we decide on our own to move in a new direction. In many situations, however, we need to seek help. Here are a few ideas to consider:

❑   Ask a trusted friend or family member for assistance.
❑   Read books that have helped others develop new approaches to their problems.
❑   Join a counseling group.
❑   Talk with a member of the clergy.
❑   Participate in a peer-support group such as Alcoholics Anonymous.
❑   Get in touch with your higher power, seek spirituality, engage in meditation and mindfulness.
❑   Consult with a licensed mental health professional.

All of these resources have proven helpful for those who are seeking to remove the blocks of their hearts and minds that have kept them from moving forward with their lives. Many have used more than one of these resources to help them rise above their Negative Core Beliefs.

FREEDOM FROM THE BLOCKS THAT TRAP US

Sabrina, Dale, and Ty successfully dealt with their previously unresolved self-beliefs. When they did this, their ineffective coping behaviors no longer held them trapped. Once released from the blocks of their hearts and minds, they could then create new ways to live their lives. By developing additional Positive Core Beliefs and a more constructive Self-Belief Identity, they created a greater measure of HEART Health Integration.

In the coming chapters, we will explore specific strategies that can be used to overcome Negative Core Beliefs and destructive coping mechanisms. These methods have worked for many people who had felt stuck in dire circumstances that were ruining the quality of their lives.

REVIEW ACTIVITY
Chapter 5

EXERCISE: What Is Blocking Me From Enjoying My Life?

PART 1: IDENTIFY YOUR INTERNAL BLOCKS

Do you ever feel like something within you is holding you back from really enjoying life? Often our blocks prevent us from feeling good about ourselves or positive about our relationships. Identify three or more of your internal blocks. Please do not list external issues such as other's problems that may affect you:

1. What is holding you back from enjoying your life more? (e.g., "Emotionally, I can't stand it when someone is disrespectful.")

2. What is another thing that is holding you back from enjoying your life more? (e.g., "I know I eat too much but I can't help myself.")

3. What is a third thing that is holding you back from enjoying your life more? (e.g., "I really want to spend more time with my partner but when I do, I often get annoyed.")

PART 2: Identify Your Emotional Triggers

Do you sometimes experience unwanted triggered emotions? We know that something is not working well when we feel overwhelmed by anger, sadness, anxiety, or fear. For example, if someone made a comment and we overreacted, then we have been emotionally triggered.

Think of the times when you have been overly MAD, SAD, or ANXIOUS. Determine if there has been any pattern to you being unduly upset, frustrated, angry, depressed, or fearful?

1.   What triggers you to overreact? (e.g., "I get mad when I'm told what to do.")

2.   What else triggers you to overreact emotionally?

3.   Are there any other triggers that cause you to overreact?

PART 3: IDENTIFY ANY HARMFUL COPING MECHANISMS THAT YOU USE

Many of us use habitual behaviors to deal with stress. Look for obsessive thoughts or repetitive behaviors that we compulsively use to escape from our Negative Core Beliefs, even though we know they provide only temporary relief. List these coping mechanisms.

1.   What do you do that is ineffective coping? (e.g., "I escape by watching too much TV.")

2.   What else do you do that is ineffective coping?

3.   Is there anything else that is ineffective coping?

You can print out each Chapter Review Activity under the Activities tab at
KeyCoreBeliefs.org. At the end of most of the Chapter Review Activities,
you'll find a link to additional activities that are available without cost.

NOTES: Use this page to record any thoughts about blocking your heart and mind—and removing the blocks.

CHAPTER 6

BUILDING SELF-BELIEF IDENTITY

Creating a Constructive Sense of Self

*It does not matter how slowly you go
as long as you do not stop.*

Confucius

HOW DO WE TRANSFORM NEGATIVE CORE BELIEFS TO BUILD OUR SELF-BELIEF IDENTITY?

It is vitally important to become conscious of our Negative Core Beliefs so that we can replace those beliefs with Positive Core Beliefs. Mel's story is an example of how we can change our lives for the better.

MEL'S STORY

The first step in Mel's recovery occurred when his wife, Lisa, left him. He felt despondent, angry, and alone. Nevertheless, he understood he deserved much of the responsibility for the breakup of his marriage. He thought about this for several days but could not fully understand what had caused him to create such a mess for himself and Lisa.

Mel was brought up in a home where excellence was praised and average performance was frowned on. Understandably, he developed strong beliefs about the need to be competitive and to win. It was never all right to be less than the best, and he felt compelled to be better than everyone else. As an adult, he had all of the trappings of success—a great job, a big pickup, a wonderful home, and a beautiful wife—until, without warning, Lisa opted out of their marriage. To make matters worse, she was the second wife to walk out on him. When she did, his life began to crumble.

Mel knew that working long hours made him a lot of money, and he was a great worker whom others relied on to fix any problem. However, he paid the price when he went home. Much like at work, Mel expected to take care of all his family's problems. He believed he was too busy to partner with Lisa, so instead he gave her "helpful and detailed instructions" on how to do just about everything.

After three years of this, Lisa ran into Mel's first wife and they started to compare notes. Not surprisingly, they discovered each of them had experienced the same pattern—Mel told them what to do and then got upset when his expectations were not met. Often, he became sarcastically angry, which led to bitter arguments about trivial matters. Because Lisa was no longer willing to put up with this, she walked out.

Fortunately, she also recognized a number of Mel's positive qualities and she wanted to build a wonderful marriage. Therefore, she decided to propose a possible reconciliation if he would seek help. Although she knew of nothing very traumatic in Mel's life, Lisa thought the unreasonable demands he placed on himself and others might be related to some experiences that she did not know about.

Shortly after Lisa left Mel, they met over coffee to talk about the possibility of reconciling. She suggested it might be helpful to talk with their minister, Carlyle. Desperate to save his marriage, he made an appointment for the next day.

During their visit, Mel poured out his story to Carlyle. Despite all his accomplishments, life seemed to create a never-ending series of new problems to solve. He felt everyone expected him to be the best at fixing things. He always had to come up with the right answers and he was good at it, but in his own mind, never good enough.

Mel had sought out his minister for two conflicting reasons. The first was to prove there was nothing really wrong with him. From his viewpoint, if only his wife had been more loving and understanding (and more compliant with his expectations), everything would have been just fine. The second was to avoid looking like he had failed at marriage again. This second failure was emotionally unacceptable to Mel.

Carlyle could see through Mel's denial of responsibility. He told Mel that effective marriage relationships require couples to partner with each other. A partnership occurs when both individuals act together to create a better life than either of them could by themselves. "After all," his minister said, "isn't that the real reason we want to be in a committed relationship? A partner who is also our best friend is at the center of all terrific marriages."

The words hit home. Mel desperately wanted to understand this more completely. Carlyle asked him if he would like to continue meeting and Mel quickly agreed. After three meetings with his minister, Mel began to see how he had been chasing his parents' desire for him to always be his best. They were good parents, but they had been disappointed whenever he had not excelled at school. Mel knew there was no point in blaming his mom and dad, however, he hoped to learn more about himself so he could better understand how to make his life fulfilling both at home and at work.

Mel began to understand how two Negative Core Beliefs had affected his sense of worth. The first was, "I am never good enough." The second belief was even more dreadful for him. He hated saying it but he believed, "I am flawed!" As Mel competed to be the best, he never achieved perfection and so he knew he always could have done better. For him, anything less than perfection equaled "flawed." This was not rational, but Negative Core Beliefs are not based on reason because they rely on partial truths.

Predictably, Mel's two Negative Core Beliefs led to the fear that there was something inherently wrong with him. When his first wife divorced him, she provided the evidence that he was unworthy to be loved. After Lisa left, he was convinced of his own worst fears and felt absolutely helpless to change.

These fears had existed since he was a child. Over time, they became evermore entrenched. It was relatively easy for him to identify that he was not good enough, but uncovering the subconscious fear, "I am flawed," was a revelation. He recognized this Negative Core Belief had been a constant companion throughout his life. Being not good enough meant he had to outperform everyone else—including Lisa. As he saw the good in her and others, he constantly compared himself with them and he never measured up. When he yelled at Lisa for not doing something "the right way," his anger proved how defective he really was. This meant he had to fool everybody into believing that he was a good person. Trying to constantly deceive others was a huge burden for him to carry.

How did this occur? Mel may never know for sure, but it might have been because as a child, he was always encouraged to "do his best." This phrase had a hidden meaning for him—it signified that he had to "be the best." Throughout his school years he applied himself by being the best student, the athlete with the most school records, and the most popular guy. However, Mel could not be the best at everything.

For example, in fifth grade he tried out for a class play but wasn't selected. This was extremely embarrassing for a child who had to be the best at everything. Mel was so ashamed about his failure that he hid it from his mom and dad. When his father learned about the play and asked him why he did not have a part, Mel lied. He said that he had been busy working on an extra-credit assignment during the tryouts and his dad believed him. Lying was a destructive coping mechanism that he mistakenly thought worked well, so he continued to lie in order to get out of any situation in which he was not the best.

As a coping mechanism, lying is a skill that can be honed to near perfection. Mel used deceit to keep others off balance so he could stay in control. His lies were subtle and used sparingly so he was rarely caught. Even when he was caught, he found he could manipulate himself out of most situations. Oddly enough, this became a source of pride but it also confirmed, "I am defective."

Being dishonest had a terrible consequence. Despite the fact that he was successful in deceiving others, this also meant Mel was "defective" because his lying went against his deeply held value to be honest. His lying was like a heavy weight that he carried everywhere, but he felt stuck with this terrible coping mechanism. He knew he was undeniably a fraud. To cover this up, he always had to be right. It was no wonder that he had no time to create a partnership with anyone, including his wife.

Once Mel exchanged his shame-based Negative Core Beliefs for Positive Core Beliefs, he was able to become more understanding of himself and others. His empathy skills increased, making it easier for him to be completely truthful in all of his dealings. For the first time in many years, he believed, "I am honest." He also discovered, "I am enough" and "I am okay."

THE POWER OF EMPATHY TO CREATE A CONSTRUCTIVE SELF-BELIEF IDENTITY

In one of their meetings, Carlyle focused Mel's attention on a highly important value. He asked Mel how he would respond to the following situation.

You are walking down a street one morning. Not many people are out. Suddenly, you see a person trip and fall down hard on the pavement. It is obvious that this person has been injured. What would you want to do in this situation?

Before reading how Mel responded, take a moment to briefly write your answer to this question: "What would you want to do if you saw a person who was seriously injured?"

After Mel answered the question, Carlyle asked, "In the future, do you imagine you would want to act the same or would you act differently?" How would you answer this question? Please write your answer.

Finally, Carlyle asked Mel, "Has there ever been a time in the past when you saw someone really hurting, and you would have not wanted to help them if you could?" Write down your answer to this question.

Of the thousands of people who have been asked these questions, it is extremely rare for a person not to care what happened to the person who had fallen. Nearly all of us have a strong desire to help another if we can. In addition, there has likely never been a time in the past when someone was hurting that we did not want to help. We might have felt helpless, but we would have wanted to be helpful. Finally, we probably cannot imagine any time in the future when we would not care about an injured person.

This capacity to emotionally understand another and then to care about them is defined as empathy. Empathy occurs when we feel happy watching a baby, when we congratulate a friend, console a person who has lost a loved one, help someone solve a problem, and in innumerable other ways. By sharing the emotion of another person's experience, we relate to them in astonishingly effective ways.

The ability to empathize is a decisively valuable interpersonal skill because it enables us to connect with other individuals. Without this sense of connection, we feel alone and isolated. Empathy is a skill that all of us can more fully develop. It is also a means to strengthen significant Positive Core Beliefs, such as, "I am caring" and "I am empathetic." These are Key Core Beliefs that crucially contribute to a constructive Self-Belief Identity.

Moreover, our development of empathy largely determines our ability to form mutually satisfying friendships and family relationships because it is so essential to understanding our loved ones. As we strive to know others, they become more important to us and we become more significant to them. This skill plays a key role in our personal development because, when we grow in our understanding of others, we learn more about ourselves.

Although almost everyone has some level of empathy, it is a skill that is too often overlooked and greatly underestimated. When we are deficient in empathy, it is a sure sign we have become more disconnected from others and therefore less effective in our interactions. If this occurs, self-doubts increase. The lack of empathy in individuals, families, organizations, cultures, and countries makes us subject to a great many fears. The results inevitably prove harmful.

Obviously, some so-called "successful" people in the world care little about others. They may amass wealth, power, or fame by climbing over others in their dog-eat-dog scramble to the top. However, as a funeral director once said, "These individuals may seem to have it all, but have you ever noticed that you never see a hearse with a roof rack?" When they die, they can't take it with them. It is interesting to speculate what these people might think about when they face the end of their lives. Fortunately, most of us don't want to live that way. In fact, we can be wonderfully successful by becoming more empathetic and caring.

The capacity and skill to identify with others is intrinsic in each of us. Children naturally empathize at a very young age. For example, they almost always empathically connect with others who are emotionally upset or physically hurting. Researchers have theorized the concept of "mirror neurons" in the brain that are activated during many of our interactions with others. If we see someone emotionally suffering, we feel related emotions. Similarly, when we see someone smiling at us, it is natural to smile in return.

DEVELOPING EMPATHY

After a few meetings with his minister, Mel realized he needed to become more empathetic. When Carlyle asked him to recall a time he had felt mad, Mel remembered an incident when he had asked Lisa to pick up a cake for an office party. She did what he had requested, but the cake was not the one he had wanted. He felt sure that Lisa simply did not care enough to get the right cake. He was furious. His minister asked Mel to identify the primary underlying feelings of his anger. When we are MAD, SAD, or ANXIOUS, one or more of the following basic feelings always underlies it. Carlyle asked if he had felt:

❑ ACCUSED: We often feel this primary feeling when we think someone is blaming or criticizing us—and we always feel accused when we accuse ourselves. Feeling self-accused is much more common than feeling accused by others.

❑ GUILTY: We feel this primary feeling when we think we did something wrong or we failed to do something we thought we should have done.

❑ REJECTED: We feel rejected if we think we have been excluded, scorned, dismissed, demeaned, ignored, or rebuffed.

❑ UNLOVABLE: This feeling occurs in close personal relationships. Because we care deeply about certain relationships, when we feel unworthy to be loved, it seems like extreme rejection. This is an especially intense feeling.

❑ POWERLESS: This particularly intense feeling occurs when we feel incapable, defenseless, vulnerable, or helpless. We cannot stand to feel powerless for long, and so we quickly try to get our power back.

All of these primary feelings occur in microseconds and only last for a few moments. When we are confronted with threatening situations, our feelings are absolutely essential for immediate "fight or flight" reactions. Because they happen so quickly, we are not consciously aware of them. However, when we reflect on any incident that caused us to be MAD, SAD, or ANXIOUS, we can always recognize that we first felt ACCUSED, GUILTY, REJECTED, UNLOVABLE, or POWERLESS, or some combination of these feelings.

To remember these underlying feelings, we use the acronym based on the first letter of each primary feeling—AGRUP™. The AGRUP feelings can be used in a four-step process to develop empathy.

The "CARE" approach

1. Consider my AGRUP feelings

Mel's minister, Carlyle, asked him to consider which of these feelings he felt when Lisa had not bought the cake that he wanted. Mel said that he felt rejected because Lisa had disregarded his wishes. In addition, he said he felt unlovable because, "If she really loved me, she would have done what I asked her." He also felt powerless because he did not have the right cake and because he could do nothing about "Lisa's mistake."

As he realized what he was saying, Mel began to understand how foolish this all sounded. Carlyle mentioned that the vast majority of our MAD, SAD, or ANXIOUS emotions are based on an inadequate understanding of ourselves, particularly when we feel ACCUSED, GUILTY, REJECTED, UNLOVABLE, and/or POWERLESS. When we fail to fully understand ourselves, we also fail to acknowledge the fundamental truth of who we are—our true nature.

2. Acknowledge my true nature

The concept of true nature has been illustrated in this chapter during the review of how we would respond to an injured person who needed help. Our true nature is central to who we are because we fundamentally care about others.

Sometimes we become too centered on ourselves and lose this perspective. Naturally, we all need to be self-aware in order to survive. For instance, when we are driving, no one is as engaged in our safety as we are. Other drivers cannot be as concerned about us because they are primarily focused on their own safety.

Paradoxically, however, all of us benefit from the safe driving of others as well as ourselves. In other words, although we need to mostly concentrate on our own welfare, we benefit ourselves and others when we also focus on their safety. To illustrate, most of us have avoided an accident by noticing another driver's unsafe action and then swerving to miss hitting the other car. Our mutual well-being depended on our safe driving as well as being concerned for the other person's safety.

Our true nature—being mindful of others—should never be disregarded. Periodically, we need to acknowledge this Key Core Belief—"I am caring." Mel considered whether or not he really was a caring person. Carlyle discussed a number of incidents that Mel had shared about others he loved and cared about. Then Carlyle asked him, "Despite some lapses when you have been overly self-centered, doesn't this demonstrate that you care about others and want the best for them? Isn't this your true nature?"

Most of us know about these two aspects of ourselves, sometimes referred to as "feeding the positive wolf" or "feeding the negative wolf." If we acknowledge our true nature more often, we feed and sustain our caring self. Mel was about to learn how to do this through empathy.

3. Respond with empathy

Carlyle asked Mel to recall again when Lisa got the cake for him, then asked, "How do think Lisa felt when she learned you were upset about what she had done?" Mel remembered how hurt she had become.

But Carlyle particularly wanted to know which of the five primary AGRUP feelings Mel thought Lisa had experienced. Mel said that he was very sure that Lisa had felt ACCUSED. He was less certain if she felt GUILTY for not getting "the right cake" because he now realized that he had not specifically said what kind of cake he wanted. However, he was convinced that she felt REJECTED and UNLOVABLE. Instead of thanking her for getting the cake, he had been angry with her. He also recognized how POWERLESS she must have felt for trying to do something positive that had turned out to be awful. She had felt helpless to stop his anger.

Envisioning Lisa's emotions enabled Mel to empathize with her. When he did this, his perception of the event completely changed. Now that he could better understand how she had experienced the cake incident, he was able to move forward to explore possible resolutions.

4. EXPLORE OUR MUTUAL BEST INTERESTS

After he considered his own AGRUP feelings, acknowledged his true nature, and had responded with empathy to understand Lisa's feelings—he was ready to learn how to create new, more constructive results.

We do this by creating a solution that would work for both the other person and ourselves. For example, Mel had never apologized to Lisa for getting angry about "the wrong cake." He now saw he obviously needed to make an apology. This could benefit Lisa and would also be worthwhile for himself.

Mel also recognized that he needed to develop ways to avoid these kinds of misunderstandings in the future. Carlyle asked Mel how this approach might work more effectively for Lisa and for himself. He decided to find out by first apologizing to Lisa and then talking over how he could more effectively communicate with her so that he could better understand her thoughts and feelings.

Communicating with openness and consideration is one way to explore our mutual best interests. If we discover what would genuinely work for both individuals, then we create a "win-win" outcome. However, if the solution only works for one person, the results will be a "win-lose," which inevitably becomes a "lose-lose" outcome. If one person wins and the other person feels disadvantaged, resentment will follow and this will lead to future problems in which the winner eventually loses.

Creating our mutual best interests requires individuals to genuinely understand each other. True partnering produces better interactions and more effective outcomes. As someone once said, "If it really is a 'win-win,' what have I got to lose?"

Sometimes coming up with a solution for both individuals is difficult, especially with time or distance from the original problem. For example, if we had a blow-out with a friend we have lost track of, what can we do to create a positive outcome? Even in these circumstances, we can still use this "mutual best interests" approach. For example, we might merely change an unhappy memory now that we have a better understanding, and we could offer our silent best wishes or some other pleasant expression of caring. We could also provide a kindness to another person. We each have many opportunities to show that we care.

As we will discuss in Chapter 11, "INSPIRED SOLUTIONS: The Vitality of Forgiveness and Transcendence," forgiveness can be a healing way to demonstrate that we are caring. The approach illustrated below can be applied in forgiving others and in finding forgiveness for ourselves. However, this topic needs to be fully considered in that chapter.

A SUMMARY OF "CARE"

The approach used by Mel's minister is referred to as "CARE." To review:

1. CONSIDER MY AGRUP FEELINGS: Did I feel ACCUSED, GUILTY, REJECTED, UNLOVABLE, POWERLESS, or some combination of these underlying primary feelings?

2. ACKNOWLEDGE MY TRUE NATURE: I remember that I am caring and I am worthy to be loved.

3. RESPOND WITH EMPATHY: How did the other person feel? Did he or she feel ACCUSED, GUILTY, REJECTED, UNLOVABLE, POWERLESS, or some combination of these feelings?

4. EXPLORE OUR MUTUAL BEST INTERESTS: What can I do to create a better, win-win outcome that truly works for both of us?

All of us can develop the skill of empathy to higher levels by repeatedly using the "CARE" approach. When we do this, we connect more fully with others and we more fully understand own feelings and thoughts. The strength of our Key Core Beliefs increases and we become more confident in our Self-Belief Identity.

Mel learned how to make the "CARE" approach a regular aspect of improving his relationships and enhancing his sense of worthy individuality.

THE "CARE" CHALLENGE

When Carlyle asked if Mel would be willing to accept a challenge that would realize the full benefits of the "CARE" approach, Mel eagerly agreed.

The purpose of the challenge was to strengthen the Key Core Beliefs of "I am worthy to be loved" and "I am caring." Carlyle emphasized that our ability to empathize with others relies on these two beliefs. Mel did not fully understand what his minister was saying, but he was assured that this exercise had empowered many individuals to transform their lives. People who faced unhappy relationships or other dire circumstances had used the "CARE" challenge to greatly develop the skill of empathy and to create a much more positive Self-Belief Identity.

The "CARE" challenge is a training program for our minds. By repetitively doing a simple exercise 12 times a day, anyone can learn how to understand others and themselves. Each exercise takes a little more than a minute to complete.

Mel was asked to begin every exercise by recalling an experience in which he had a problem with another person. It could have been any recent event or any experience from his past. Next, he was to work through each of the four steps of "CARE." He was asked to first, consider his AGRUP feelings, second, acknowledge his true nature, third, respond with empathy for the other person's AGRUP feelings, and fourth, explore one or more mutual best interests.

These exercises can be done while driving a car, shopping for groceries, or at any other convenient time. Mel agreed to do this exercise 12 times each day. He had reminder notes on his mirror in the bathroom, on the refrigerator, and in his car. Every time he saw a note, he worked through three or four events. If he could not think of an event, Carlyle told him he could repeat an incident that he had already processed as long as he completed each of the four steps. The daily repetition became his program for advanced empathy training.

Mel used the "CARE" exercises to process any current problems or any old unresolved experiences. After putting the approach into daily practice, he found that he could work through these experiences in just one or two minutes. One after the other, he took the time to resolve all of his past hurts and upsetting memories. In a few weeks, longstanding problematic experiences and resentments had been transformed and they never troubled him again. Just as significantly, he gained new perspectives on his present relationships and strengthened his Positive Core Beliefs.

Since many of the experiences Mel remembered occurred a number of years ago, he was counseled to devise a simple way to create "mutual best interest" outcomes. Mel chose to offer a good thought or a prayer on behalf of the person. He made a note of any events that continued to trouble him or that could not easily be resolved, so that he and Carlyle could review them in their next meeting. However, with this new means of understanding his feelings and using empathy to understand the feelings of others, Mel discovered that he could readily resolve nearly all of his past negative experiences.

Initially, the "CARE" challenge wasn't easy for Mel, and it's not easy for many others. Despite the fact that it usually totally takes no more than 20 minutes a day to do the 12 exercises, those of us with strong Negative Core Beliefs may find these exercises quite difficult. Sometimes it takes a week or two to get into the rhythm of doing "CARE," but it soon becomes enjoyable and meaningful.

The first week, Mel followed his minister's recommendation to record on a note card the number of times each day he completed the "CARE" process. On the first day, he did all 12 of the exercises. The next day he again did the exercise 12 times. On the third day, Mel did not remember the exercises until late in the day but he completed eight of them just before he went to bed. The next day, he recorded doing all 12 exercises. But on the fifth day he totally forgot. When he remembered, he said to himself, "Who am I kidding. It is ridiculous to believe that I am ever going to get Lisa back. Why should I even try? This whole thing is a waste."

Mel's Negative Core Beliefs reasserted themselves and he became discouraged. When he next met with his minister, he was embarrassed to admit he had given up.

His minister was neither disappointed nor surprised. Counting up his efforts, he noted Mel had completed 44 out of the possible 84 exercises for the week. Carlyle said that others had similar experiences. However, he told Mel that everyone has the ability to complete the exercises of the "CARE" challenge and encouraged Mel to try again.

Mel did the exercises for the next seven days and reported that he did all of the 84 possible exercises! It was just a beginning, but he felt good about himself and he unfailingly continued to do the exercises for the next six weeks.

It may not seem logical that repeatedly doing a relatively simple activity will change our lives. However, many people have found the "CARE" challenge to be an essential first step in gaining a greater sense of peace and personal fulfilment. They begin to hope and then to believe, "I am worthy to be loved."

Gray, one of the coauthors of this book, related his own experience with the "CARE" approach.

GRAY'S EXPERIENCE

Sometimes people ask me how I became a mental health professional. It all started with a problem that had plagued me for most of my adult life. I was annoyed much of the time and often angry with my circumstances. I did not know it then but I frequently felt ACCUSED, UNLOVABLE, and POWERLESS.

Then a friend of mine, who was a mental health professional, introduced me to the "CARE" challenge that helped me become more empathetic. As I daily did the exercises to work through my life experiences, I began to get a much clearer understanding of my past and current relationships. This, in turn, helped me to greatly recognize a number of my Negative Core Beliefs and to then develop favorable self-beliefs. During this time, the Key Core Beliefs of "I am caring" and "I am worthy to be loved" also enriched my Self-Belief Identity. I began to see myself much more positively.

This approach was so effective that I was able to develop new, productive patterns of feeling, thinking, and behaving. As I realized these benefits, it gave me the confidence to move in new life directions. Eventually, I went back to graduate school to complete the requirements to become licensed as a Clinical Mental Health Counselor. If I could do it, anyone can.

Approaches such as "CARE" have helped thousands develop the skill of empathy. It works because consistent daily practice, 12 times a day, retrains our brains. By becoming more empathetic, people have redirected the course of their lives. It does take effort, but "CARE" achieves amazing results. However, please do not be discouraged if you find it difficult to do the first few weeks. Persistence will create great rewards.

EFFECTIVELY RESOLVING PAST EXPERIENCES

Although many of us have spent years accumulating the evidence that our Negative Core Beliefs are true, it does not take an equal period of time to reverse these beliefs. We can substantially change our beliefs in about seven weeks of focused attention. As we do this, we are making new neurological connections. These connections can be further strengthened by continuing our efforts for another five weeks. The key to the success in this exercise is to consistently concentrate our minds 12 times a day, every day, for at least seven weeks.

Although the amount of required time varies from person to person, most individuals will notice significant positive changes in the first four weeks. Consistent, daily practice creates the conditions for brain-retraining. Athletes know that concentrated practice can greatly improve their performance in a relatively short time. All of us learn new skills in much the same way. How long, for example, did it take to get comfortable with a different software program, learn how to get around in a new town, learn how to keyboard, or develop a new hobby or sport?

To form added capabilities requires consistent and focused effort. We all know there are no shortcuts to learning. However, if we are willing to steadily work at it, we can transform Negative Core Beliefs into a Positive Core Beliefs in a matter of weeks. Our old patterns of thinking and feeling will change.

Mel continued doing the exercises, and Carlyle showed him added ways to strengthen his belief that he was "worthy to be loved." This will be explored more completely in the next chapter. Finally, he worked with Mel to help him resolve some of the other Negative Core Beliefs that were troubling him. For example, he helped him learn the difference between "being the best" and "doing well." Mel began to understand he could let go of his perfectionist expectations. In just a few weeks, he recognized, "I am good enough," a wonderfully encouraging change in his Self-Belief Identity.

After seeing the progress Mel was making, his wife began to have hope for their marriage. Lisa and Mel talked over ways they could restart their relationship based on genuine friendship. For the first time, they each started to see each other as a real partner. It was a new beginning for both of them.

Empathy is vital to unlocking the Key Core Beliefs of "I am caring" and "I am worthy to be loved." When we focus on being more empathetic, we more fully realize our inherent strengths and abilities. Our Self-Belief Identity becomes positively reflected in the distinctive nature of who we are. As our relationships improve, we experience the benefits of Health Integration and greater Core-Related Health (Chapter 2).

WHEN TO SEEK TREATMENT FROM PROFESSIONALS WITH SPECIAL TRAINING

If an individual has a history of unresolved trauma, chronic distress, anxiety, unexplained fears or phobias, or any other continuing psychological concerns including depression, this person may want to consider seeing a specialist. Some licensed mental health professionals and some ministers are specially trained to resolve traumatic and chronically distressful experiences. They usually have postgraduate training in treating trauma and anxiety.

Those who specialize in dealing with these conditions may not use the approaches described in this book. Nevertheless, they can be very effective in helping people work through any underlying Negative Core Beliefs. It is a good idea to ask about their training in treating anxiety or trauma. Don't be afraid to inquire about their effectiveness in relieving distress for their former clients.

More information on this topic is available in APPENDIX C: "Finding a Qualified Mental Health Professional."

REVIEW ACTIVITY
Chapter 6

Please consider the following questions:

Referring back to the questions in this chapter on helping an injured person, how did you answer those questions? How could you more fully develop the skill of empathy? For example, some individuals focus on becoming a better listener or more understanding of others' feelings. How would you improve these skills?

How would developing a higher level of empathy be important for your relationships? Empathy has been referred to as the most essential skill for personal and professional success. You may want to explore how this might apply to you, your family relationships, and your other life experiences.

Can you visualize an interaction with a person who strengthens your sense that "I am worthy to be loved?" Frequently, experiences with children are most helpful because children do not have agendas and their feelings are genuine. As you acknowledge your true nature, you may want to picture a loving interaction with a child as a powerful way to prove that you are love-worthy.

How helpful would it be for you to do the exercise that Mel did? If you decide to do this, make a firm commitment with yourself to follow through for at least seven consecutive weeks. It takes daily practice for the brain to make new neural connections and for the results to be noticeable. You may want to consider working with someone who will encourage you, such as a friend, family member, member of the clergy, etc.

Before leaving this chapter, please read the poem, "Children Learn What They Live" on the next page. The ideas in this poem emphasize the crucial self-beliefs that many of us as children internalized. If Negative Core Beliefs were formed, we can transform them into constructive beliefs. If Positive Core Beliefs were formed, we can further strengthen them.

CHILDREN LEARN WHAT THEY LIVE

If children live with criticism, they learn to condemn.

If children live with hostility, they learn to fight.

If children live with fear, they learn to be apprehensive.

If children live with pity, they learn to feel sorry for themselves.

If children live with ridicule, they learn to be shy.

If children live with jealousy, they learn what envy is.

If children live with shame, they learn to feel guilty.

If children live with tolerance, they learn to be patient.

If children live with encouragement, they learn to be confident.

If children live with praise, they learn to appreciate.

If children live with approval, they learn to like themselves.

If children live with acceptance, they learn to find love in the world.

If children live with recognition, they learn to have a goal.

If children live with sharing, they learn to be generous.

If children live with honesty and fairness, they learn what truth and justice are.

If children live with security, they learn to have faith in themselves
and in those around them.

If children live with friendliness, they learn that the world is a nice place
in which to live.

If children live with serenity, they learn to have peace of mind.

With what are your children living?

DOROTHY LAW NOLTE (1924–2005)
WRITER AND FAMILY COUNSELOR (1993 VERSION)

You can print out each Chapter Review Activity under the Activities tab at
KeyCoreBeliefs.org. At the end of most of the Chapter Review Activities,
you'll find a link to additional activities that are available without cost.

NOTES: Use this page to record any thoughts about building your Self-Belief Identity through increased empathy.

CHAPTER 7

THE COMPLETE PERSON

A Recipe for Life Success

Challenging the meaning of life
is the truest expression of the state of being human.

Viktor E. Frankl

HOW CAN WE CREATE A SENSE OF WHOLENESS?

The sense of self, our Self-Belief Identity, is based on four interrelated basics.

THE BASICS OF SELF-BELIEF IDENTITY

❑ BELIEVE: "I am worthy to be loved, and I have predominantly Positive Core Beliefs."

❑ UNDERSTAND: "I know my feelings and how to regulate my emotions."

❑ CONNECT: "I continually build caring relationships."

❑ IMAGINE: "I visualize and value the meaning of my life."

When one of these four basics of Self-Belief Identity is diminished, the other three will also decline. In all of the previous stories that we have reviewed, each of the individual's self-beliefs were embedded in the most fundamental Negative Core Belief, "I am unworthy to be loved." For those who genuinely believe this, their understanding of their feelings is reduced, their connections with others are reduced, and they have less ability to imagine the meaning of their lives. When this happens, life is out of balance and self-worth is diminished.

In Chapter 6, Mel recognized that he did not BELIEVE he was worthy to be loved. But he likewise knew he had almost no ability to UNDERSTAND his feelings and how to regulate them. When his wife, Lisa, left him, he realized he had made little effort to truly CONNECT with her and he rarely had any real connection with others. In addition, Mel had been in the fast lane at work for so long, he had no real vision of his future and could not IMAGINE either a successful marriage or a meaningful life. Mel felt his life was unbalanced. He did not feel whole.

THE DIFFERENCE BETWEEN SELF-WORTH AND SELF-ESTEEM

In this book we make an important distinction between our self-esteem and our self-worth. Self-esteem is based on the feedback we receive from others that we find believable. If someone compliments us and we believe them, our self-esteem goes up a degree. On the other hand, when someone gives us negative feedback and we believe what that person says, our self-esteem decreases. For example, if someone says, "You probably could have taken better care of that situation," many people would feel their self-esteem drop.

Feedback from other people helps us understand how they view our behaviors. Their perspectives are often valuable in reviewing our own effectiveness. However, sometimes their perspectives and feedback may be quite inaccurate. Regardless of the degree of accuracy, the important question is whether or not we believe the feedback. If a child is "constructively criticized" for doing poorly in school, he or she will almost certainly experience a decline in self-esteem.

By contrast, if a child does poorly on a math test, he or she might say, "When it comes to math, I am dumb." This self-message could develop into a Negative Core Belief and become a measure of self-worth. In other words, what others say and we believe impacts our self-esteem. What we say and believe about ourselves impacts our self-worth.

While feedback from others can be helpful, what we say and believe about ourselves is much more important. Self-esteem can contribute to forming self-worth. However, regardless of what others say, our self-worth is predominant because it is based on who we believe we really are. Our Negative and Positive Core Beliefs and Self-Belief Identity are directly related to our own internal sense of self-worth.

CAPTURING A NEW VISION OF OURSELVES

When we have low self-worth and feel out of balance, we are also anxious. Our ability to be mentally effective is reduced because anxiety adversely impacts our cognitive reasoning. Most often, our relationships with others also become diminished. Additionally, this can reduce our resistance to infections or in other ways degrade our health. As noted in Chapter 1, the quality of our HEALTH, our mental AWARENESS, our EMOTIONS, our RELATIONSHIPS, and our TRANSCENDENCE are all interrelated.

On the other hand, the basics of Self-Belief Identity can powerfully work to create a personal sense of wholeness. They can help us chart the course of our lives. We can harness them to strengthen our ability to BELIEVE, UNDERSTAND, CONNECT, and IMAGINE. When we know how to focus our attention on these basics, we develop greater capacity to use the skills that are most vital to our success. We also increase our self-worth and Positive Core Beliefs and feel more whole or complete.

We cannot become truly successful and be confident in our self-worth until we UNDERSTAND our feelings, CONNECT with others in caring relationships, and IMAGINE how to appreciate the meaning of our lives. These three elements support and strengthen our ability to BELIEVE that we are worthy of love.

In the last chapter, Mel thought that he was successful. His myth exploded when Lisa left him. For a while he blamed her. He even started to blame all women for his problems. Fortunately, Mel's minister gave him the support he needed to see that the only block to his mind, heart, and soul had been himself.

With this understanding came a new awareness. By talking with Lisa, his minister, friends, colleagues, and others, Mel started to learn how to replace old patterns of perceiving, feeling, thinking, and behaving with more effective abilities. He discovered what worked. It only took a few months for Mel to recognize how he could move his life forward in ways he never before could have conceived.

He started by systematically converting his negative beliefs into Positive Core Beliefs by becoming aware of his AGRUP feelings (ACCUSED, GUILTY, REJECTED, UNLOVABLE, and/or POWERLESS), strengthening his true nature, practicing empathy, and exploring mutual best interests. With consistent effort, he began to BELIEVE that he was worthy to be loved. He also learned how to apply the concepts presented in the next chapters, in order to more fully UNDERSTAND his emotions. He conscientiously endeavored to improve his relationships at work and with his family to CONNECT with others. Mel also began to IMAGINE a more meaningful future opening up before him. The Self-Belief Identity basics—BELIEVE, UNDERSTAND,

CONNECT, and IMAGINE—initiated the beginnings of a more complete sense of himself.

As he strengthened the basics of his Self-Belief Identity, Mel's Positive Core Beliefs increased. In addition, his confidence in his self-worth improved. He was developing a growing sense of wholeness. Months later he told his minister that he could see himself positively for the first time because he was living his life wholeheartedly.

Mel realized what sages throughout history have known: We are the authors of our own life stories. Our success relies on the basics of Self-Belief Identity that work together for us—or against us. It is left to each of us to determine the story that we will write. We may well ask ourselves, "What is the story I am creating?" Emily's account illustrates how numerous life challenges can become constructive if we are willing to apply the Self-Belief Identity basics.

EMILY'S STORY

Raised by a single mother who was chronically ill and debilitated, Emily tried her best to take care of her mom and her younger brother and sister. By the time she turned 14, she was responsible for shopping, cooking, helping her siblings with homework, and everything else her mother needed her to do. Although this was challenging, Emily was proud that she helped out at home, still managed to earn excellent grades in school, and had a number of good friends.

After graduating from high school, Emily wanted to become an accountant so she attended a local community college while continuing to take care of her sister and brother. She also worked as a bookkeeper to provide added income for the family. As she finished her first year of college, Emily met Roger. He was four years older and making an outstanding income in sales. In addition, he was both charming and good-looking. Roger was attracted to Emily because she was a hard worker, reliable, and pretty. Her friends and family were excited when Emily and Roger announced their engagement.

Planning for her wedding had been a blur. Roger's mother stepped in and decided most of the details. Three months after they first met, Emily walked down the aisle to say "I do." She hoped their marriage would be a wonderful, life-long partnership, but this was not to be.

. Shortly after the honeymoon, Roger became insistent that Emily comply with his wishes. Her life now became centered on his demands for house-keeping and meals, her appearance, and fulfilling his sexual expectations.

At first, Emily was thrilled to make her husband feel loved and appre-ciated. However, she quickly discovered that she could never fully satisfy his exacting expectations. Roger did not want her working, so she lost contact with her previous work associates. Because he insisted that his friends must be her friends, she felt isolated from almost everyone she had known. Just before their first anniversary, Emily discovered she was pregnant. Rather than rejoicing in this news, Roger and his mother couldn't understand why she had not waited for two or three years.

Although as a teenager she had been used to stressful family circum-stances, the anxieties of her marriage soon became overwhelming. Her anxiety contributed to a number of health concerns related to her preg-nancy. Also, she inadvertently learned Roger had been compulsively engaged in video pornography for many years. When this problem became an open issue, she was blamed by Roger and his mother for not taking care of her husband's sexual needs.

By the time their son was born, Emily questioned her competence, her intelligence, and her sanity. Two months later, Roger sued for divorce and sole custody of their child. He had a good friend who was an experienced divorce attorney and Emily was terrified her child would be taken from her. Shortly after filing for divorce, Roger's mother made a complaint to Child Protective Services, and an investigator opened an inquiry regarding Emily's fitness as a parent. Her self-worth plummeted. She became petrified that her worst fears would become real.

Alone, frightened, and feeling physically weak, Emily visited her obste-trician. She told her doctor that she felt like she was going crazy. Her doctor noted significant changes in Emily's emotional well-being and referred her to a licensed mental health professional, Byron, who was a trauma specialist. In their first meeting, Byron assured Emily of her sanity and intelligence.

After listening to the history of her childhood and early adulthood, he also said she was remarkably resilient. However, he thought Emily would benefit from weekly counseling that included helping her find the resources to successfully navigate the divorce and the child-custody proceedings.

Few of us have had to deal with the specific problems that Emily faced. However, most of us will occasionally be confronted with overwhelming emotional experiences. When we have to face an unexpected set of circumstances that is highly disturbing and distressing, it affects our Self-Belief Identity because it reduces our ability to:

❑ BELIEVE. We no longer feel as assured that we are worthy to be loved. Until she met with her mental health professional, Emily was convinced that there was something seriously wrong with her and that she did not deserve to be loved.

❑ UNDERSTAND. When we are emotionally overwhelmed, we don't trust our feelings and we lose our ability to regulate our emotions. During her marriage, Emily was in a relentless state of anxiety. She lived in constant fear of displeasing Roger and was always afraid that she would lose control and make a fool of herself in front of others.

❑ CONNECT. If we feel psychologically beleaguered, we have much more difficulty maintaining positive relationships. For Emily, this meant feeling isolated from friends and family who would have supported her. She felt trapped in what she thought was a prison of her own making.

❑ IMAGINE. If our life has little meaning, we may lose a lot of our ability to visualize positive solutions. Emily had no faith in her future. Although she greatly loved her son, she fully expected he would be taken from her.

These circumstances breed Negative Core Beliefs that reflect poor self-worth. In most of these situations, our Self-Belief Identity is diminished and we feel less whole. In Emily's state of affairs, she could not comprehend how her husband had become so dissatisfied with her. She was sure she was totally unworthy of love and blamed herself for their problems. Working with Byron, Emily learned how to see herself and others more accurately.

For example, Emily had been convinced by Roger that she was an incompetent mother. Byron asked her how much she loved her son. She almost became indignant and quickly responded that it was not possible to measure the love she had for her little boy. Byron then asked to what extent would Emily go to protect her child, nurture him, and make sure he was loved. As she answered this question, she grasped how much her son needed her. Instead of allowing her husband to take custody, Emily began to see her role as a mother who was fighting for the best interests of her child. Her previous Negative Core Belief of "I am unfit as a mother" became the strong Positive Core Belief of "I am a loving, caring mother! My baby needs me."

In her marriage, both her husband and mother-in-law were highly disapproving of Emily. Because they had criticized her so often, Emily had started to believe that their criticisms must be true. Her self-esteem and self-worth plunged. She developed a number of new Negative Core Beliefs that needed to be identified and converted to Positive Core Beliefs. After a few months of diligent effort, she found that her strengths and abilities empowered her to persist and to be effective despite the problems of her divorce.

As she gained greater self-worth, Emily made sensible decisions regarding the divorce settlement and the custody of her son. Her former husband never let up in his endless efforts to demean and take advantage of her. However, she came to see him as a troubled individual who was dominated by an insecure mother. It was apparent that he had very poor coping skills and an enormous sense of entitlement. Emily learned how to withstand his mental assaults as she became ever surer of her worth and her Positive Core Beliefs. She became more whole.

Emily's experience shows how many of us need specific support in overcoming trauma, chronic distress, or any intense problematic conditions. For example, if any of us were injured with a broken leg, we would want the help of a skilled doctor such as an orthopedic surgeon. Only a qualified physician would have the necessary training and skill to reset the bone and cast our leg so it would heal properly and allow us to eventually regain full mobility. Obviously, we would not delay seeking medical care for a month or even for a few days.

Likewise, during times of unrelenting distress, most of us will need the skilled services of a mental health professional or other specialist who can help us resolve our Negative Core Beliefs. When this happens, we need to find a professional who can address our concerns and help us develop Positive Core Beliefs in order to gain a greater sense of self-worth. As we appreciate the power of undesirable beliefs and the capability we have to change them, we can work through any concern when we have the needed support.

The five essentials of Health Integration—HEART (HEALTH, EMOTIONS, AWARENESS, RELATIONSHIPS, and TRANSCENDENCE)—include the ability to see ourselves as healthy individuals. When we pay attention to our physical wellness and our emotional well-being, we become stronger and more resilient. As our Positive Core Beliefs grow, we become more WORTHY, ACCEPTABLE, and CAPABLE (WAC). We also experience better Health Integration and a more harmonious balance of the basics of Self-Belief Identity:

I BELIEVE:
I am worthy to be loved.
I have predominantly Positive Core Beliefs.
When I become aware of Negative Core Beliefs,
    I am confident in my ability to transform them.
Overall, I am at peace with myself.

I UNDERSTAND:
I know my feelings and how to regulate my emotions.
I have an emotional vocabulary to identify how I feel.
When I am angry, sad, or anxious, I create a desirable
    emotional state by soothing self-care or
    constructive interactions with others.
I appreciate my negative emotions as indicators for
    self-assessment and improvement.

I CONNECT:
I continually build caring relationships.
I acknowledge the importance of my loved ones
    by positively interacting with them.
I value other individuals, but I do not overly depend
    on anyone.
I continually work to create relationships based on
    our mutual best interests.

I IMAGINE:
I value the meaning of my life.
My life has significance to myself and others.
I look for ways to create purpose in my daily experiences.
I visualize how to navigate through challenges.
I create a climate of continuous learning and
    personal development.

When we BELIEVE, UNDERSTAND, CONNECT, and IMAGINE, we create the foundation of all truly successful human endeavors. As we develop these basics, we create a stronger sense of wholeness in ourselves.

All of us have the basics of Self-Belief Identity to some degree, but they can be improved to create greater Core-Related Health. In the coming chapter, we will review how to enlarge our capabilities to create added enjoyment and greater self-worth.

REVIEW ACTIVITY
Chapter 7

Before reading the next chapter, please consider answering the questions in the following exercise regarding self-worth:

THE SELF-WORTH REVIEW: How do you value your self-worth? Our self-worth relies on our Key Core Beliefs and is directly related to our Self-Belief Identity.

Directions: For each of the statements below, rate these behaviors in your life. Please mark each statement using a number from the following rating scale:

1) Never   2) Rarely   3) Sometimes   4) Frequently   5) Almost always

_____ I seek approval and affirmation from others, and I am afraid of criticism.

_____ I guess at what normal behavior is, and I usually feel as if I am different from other people.

_____ I am anxious about people in authority roles.

_____ I am rarely able to appreciate my own accomplishments and good deeds.

_____ I tend to have difficulty following a project through from beginning to end.

_____ I get frightened or stressed when I am in the company of an angry person.

_____ In order to avoid a conflict, I find it easier to lie than to tell the truth.

_____ I have problems with compulsive behaviors such as drinking, drug use, self-harm, gambling, eating concerns, smoking, use of sex, unnecessary spending, etc.

_____ I am highly critical of myself. I am my own worst critic.

_____ I feel more alive in the midst of a crisis. I am uneasy when my life is going smoothly and I am continually anticipating problems.

_____ I have difficulty having fun. I don't seem to know how to relax and enjoy my life.

_____ I am attracted to others who have been victims, whom I feel sorry for. I develop close relationships with people who need me to help or rescue them.

_____ I need perfection in my life, and I often expect perfection from others.

_____ I frequently seek out novelty, excitement, and the challenge of newness in my life with little concern for possible negative consequences.

_____ I take myself very seriously, and I view all of my relationships just as seriously.

_____ I have problems developing and maintaining intimate relationships.

_____ I feel guilty when I stand up for myself or take care of my needs first. I prefer taking care of others' needs first.

_____ I seek or attract people who have compulsive behaviors (e.g., alcohol, drugs, gambling, food, shopping, sex, smoking, overworking, or seeking excitement.)

_____ I feel responsible for others and I find it easier to have concern for others than for myself.

_____ I am loyal to people for whom I care, even if their actions demonstrate that they do not deserve my loyalty.

_____ I cling to and will do anything to hold on to relationships because I am afraid of being alone or abandoned.

_____ I am impulsive. I frequently act too quickly before considering alternative actions or the possible undesirable consequences.

_____ I have difficulty expressing feelings. Sometimes, I really feel out of touch with my feelings.

_____ I often mistrust my feelings and the feelings expressed by others.

_____ I regularly isolate myself from other people. I am initially shy and withdrawn in new social settings.

_____ I belief I have been victimized, or I often feel that I am being taken advantage of by individuals or society in general.

_____ I can be exceedingly responsible much of the time, but I can be extremely irresponsible at other times.

_____ When I feel considerably stressed, I am confused, angry at myself, or not in control of my life.

_____ I spend a lot of time and energy cleaning up the messes and the negative consequences of my impulsive actions.

_____ I deny that my current problems stem from any of my past experiences. There are no unresolved issues that impede my current life.

_____ TOTAL SCORE

See the following page for information on how to interpret your results.

Scoring and interpretation

Add the scores for all 30 items. The total indicates your self-worth and wholeness.

0-30   Excellent self-worth.

31-45   Good self-worth—but consider boosting your Positive
                Core Beliefs.

46-60   Mildly low self-worth—develop additional Positive Core Beliefs.

61-90   Moderately low self-worth—learn to systematically
                recognize Negative Core Beliefs and transform them into
                Positive Core Beliefs.

91 or more   Low self-worth—request support in converting
                Negative Core Beliefs into Positive Core Beliefs

What is your reaction to the Self-Worth Review?

You can print out each Chapter Review Activity under the Activities tab at
KeyCoreBeliefs.org. At the end of most of the Chapter Review Activities,
you'll find a link to additional activities that are available without cost.

NOTES: What has been important for you to learn about the basics of Self-Belief Identity?

❑ BELIEVE: "I am worthy to be loved, and I have predominantly Positive Core Beliefs."

❑ UNDERSTAND: "I know my feelings and how to regulate my emotions."

❑ CONNECT: "I continually build caring relationships."

❑ IMAGINE: "I visualize and value the meaning of my life."

CHAPTER 8

EMOTIONAL SKILL-BUILDING

The Basis of a Life Well-Lived

There is no fear in love;
but perfect love casts out fear.

1 John 4:18, New Testament, KJV

HOW CAN EMOTIONAL REGULATION TRANSFORM MAD, SAD, AND ANXIOUS REACTIONS?

Every so often, we encounter emotionally charged situations that are very upsetting. During an argument with his wife, Dev became really frustrated and angry. Then, unexpectedly, his anger subsided. He wanted to know how this had happened.

DEV'S STORY

Dev's plans for the night had been destroyed. He and his wife, Cindy, had previously agreed to have dinner, watch a movie, and then share sexual intimacy. But Cindy had just informed him that she needed to spend the evening with her older sister who was dealing with a crisis. Dev felt he should be sympathetic because his sister-in-law, a single mom, was having a tough time raising her three boys alone. On the other hand, even though he knew Cindy was her sister's main emotional support, he was really irritated with her for suddenly changing their plans.

This was not the first time Cindy had cancelled a date in order to spend time with her sister. It did not help when Cindy sarcastically asked, "Why are you so unhappy? I will be back by 10 o'clock." This just made Dev more frustrated because he could not describe why it upset him so much. Rationally, he knew this was not a big deal, but it did not stop him from feeling very annoyed. In a matter of moments, his frustration turned to anger and he said, "Why do you always do this to me?" It was the beginning of a first-class argument.

Fortunately, the argument came to an abrupt halt when Cindy's tone of voice changed and she thoughtfully said, "I know our dates are important for us, and I can imagine you feel rejected and helpless to do anything about it. Help me understand this better, will you?"

Cindy was employing the interpersonal skill of empathy. She also used an emotional vocabulary that Dev could understand. She asked Dev to help her better understand what was really going on. As soon as this happened, Dev felt that he had been:

Heard. And understood. And accepted.

His anger immediately began to dwindle. Dev apologized for getting angry and Cindy said she was sorry her sister's problems had again interfered with their plans for a romantic evening. Together they devised a new plan to get together the following night—no matter what. What could have caused resentment and conflict became the means for this couple to resolve their concerns and create stronger bonds of love.

Before Cindy left to visit her sister, Dev considered how she had changed the nature of their disagreement and turned it around in just a few seconds. He wanted to know how she had done this. Cindy had just completed a training program at work designed to improve customer relations. After her company had received a number of complaints from regular customers, an alarmed CEO directed all employees to take an emotional skill-building workshop.

At the end of the training, the instructor said, "Effective customer relations can be applied to any circumstance, even in our families. If you don't believe me, try it out the next time you have a disagreement with a family member." After the first few moments of clashing with Dev, Cindy remembered the instructor's challenge. As she related this to Dev, he became intrigued and wanted to learn more. She brought out the training handouts and spent the next 10 minutes going over them with him before she had to leave. Since he had unexpected free time that evening while Cindy was with her sister, he took some time to better understand the concepts she had learned in her training.

What Cindy and Dev learned about emotional skill-building changed the quality of their relationship and strengthened their Positive Core Beliefs.

All of us can benefit from understanding and enhancing the primary emotional skills we already have. We can also learn how to increase our ability to effectively apply them, particularly in stressful circumstances.

Our emotional skills include a number of abilities that we use in a variety of circumstances. Everyone can achieve greater personal success by more fully developing them. Here are some of the most important skills.

BE AWARE OF OUR EMOTIONS AND OUR AGRUP FEELINGS
(AGRUP STANDS FOR ACCUSED, GUILTY, REJECTED, UNLOVABLE, AND POWERLESS)

The four basic emotional groups are:

MAD, SAD, and ANXIOUS emotions—and GLAD emotions.

All of our emotions fall within these general emotional categories. For example, if we observe our partner flirting with someone, we could experience the emotion of jealousy. Jealousy is often a combination of MAD and ANXIOUS emotions. We are MAD because our partner appears to be flirting and ANXIOUS because we might lose our partner.

Psychologists have referred to these emotions as "secondary emotions" because other "primary emotions" prompt these emotional reactions. These underlying primary feelings are universal to all humans. We discussed them in Chapter 6, but we will now become more familiar with them.

Our underlying primary feelings always precede and generate our secondary emotions. They also precede our cognitive thoughts. When we are upset, frustrated, embarrassed, hurt, depressed, worried, fearful—in any way MAD, SAD, or ANXIOUS—one or more of the unpleasant underlying primary feelings has been activated. We feel:

❑ **A**CCUSED
❑ **G**UILTY
❑ **R**EJECTED
❑ **U**NLOVABLE
❑ **P**OWERLESS

We refer to these initial emotional reactions as the AGRUP underlying primary feelings. When we are upset, we commonly experience two or more of these primary feelings. These uncomfortable primary feelings cause all of our MAD, SAD, or ANXIOUS secondary emotions. For instance, when we remember a time when we were annoyed (a MAD secondary emotion), we can readily identify if we first felt

ACCUSED, GUILTY, REJECTED, UNLOVABLE, POWERLESS, or some combination of these feelings. In the prior example of jealousy, a person who was MAD and ANXIOUS might feel REJECTED, UNLOVABLE, and POWERLESS.

We can become more aware of our MAD, SAD, ANXIOUS, or GLAD emotions and our underlying primary feelings as this chart helps to illustrate:

Emotional state:

If I am MAD, SAD, or ANXIOUS ...

AGRUP underlying primary feelings:

... I feel ACCUSED, GUILTY, REJECTED, UNLOVABLE, or POWERLESS.

Whenever we experience any of the secondary emotions, we can be certain that we have felt one or more of our primary AGRUP feelings. High-speed photography of facial muscles shows that our distinctive AGRUP feelings are reactions to our perceptions. These reactions occur in just a fraction of a second. Triggered by our senses, our feelings transpire so quickly that we are unaware of them or how they create our emotions. However, we can always recognize them when we look back at any of our past MAD, SAD, or ANXIOUS experiences. There are no exceptions.

The AGRUP feelings generate all of our negative secondary emotions. Referring back to Dev, when he learned he and Cindy would not be going out that evening together, he experienced frustration and anger. Both of these are MAD secondary emotions. Now, let's explore the underlying primary feelings that caused his anger. Did he feel ACCUSED, GUILTY, REJECTED, UNLOVABLE, or POWERLESS?

Dev reviewed the following:

❑ ACCUSED. Did he momentarily feel accused by Cindy or did he feel accused by himself?

> Dev said, "Now I see that I felt self-accused because it seemed she was more interested in spending time with her sister than with me. Therefore, I accused myself of not being very important to Cindy."

❑ GUILTY. Did he briefly feel a sense of self-reproach?

> Dev noted, "I felt guilty because I thought I should have had more compassion for Cindy's sister."

❑ REJECTED. Did he temporarily feel disregarded?

> He said, "Cindy seems to always have something more important to do than to be with me, so I felt rejected."

❑ UNLOVABLE. Did he momentarily feel unworthy to be loved?

> Dev believed, "If Cindy really loved me, she would know how important it is for us to spend time together. Although I know it doesn't make any sense, for a short while, I did feel unlovable."

❑ POWERLESS. Did he fleetingly feel helpless to do anything about Cindy's decision?

> Dev said, "I felt powerless because I knew there was nothing I could do to change her mind. Once she decided to visit her sister, it was a done deal."

Dev could have felt any combination of these feelings but in this situation, he experienced all of them in a split second even though he had no awareness of them. Because they occur so quickly, it is crucial to emphasize that we are almost never conscious of our underlying primary feelings. At the time, Dev knew he was upset, but he had no understanding of his feelings and he had no ability to describe them in words. However, when he later considered his AGRUP feelings, he said he could readily recognize each of them.

Our feelings exist only for brief moments before we instantly move on to whatever occurs next in our emotions and thoughts. But these feelings are always there, just below our conscious awareness. If we stop to analyze any of our emotions, we can easily identify the linked AGRUP underlying primary feelings.

As noted in Chapter 3, our Key Core Beliefs act as filters to our activating perceptions. When we have an activating perception, it passes through our Key Core Belief filters and we then feel one or more underlying feelings. These feelings create our emotions, and our emotions strongly influence our thoughts and actions. The chain reaction goes like this:

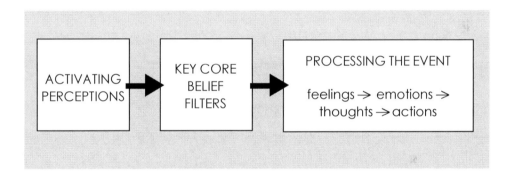

Therefore, our feelings are distinctively specific for each of us in every one of our experiences. Dev felt ACCUSED, GUILTY, REJECTED, UNLOVABLE, and POWERLESS about his situation, but someone else in the same situation could have felt any or none of those feelings.

Once Cindy recognized that he was upset, she tried to understand Dev's possible feelings when she said, "I know our dates are important to you and I imagine you might feel rejected and helpless to do anything about it. Help me understand this better, will you?"

She was guessing, of course, but her attempt to empathize with Dev created an atmosphere of emotional support. This proved to be a turning point for Dev and Cindy and, instead of an argument, they came up with a solution.

CREATE MORE POSITIVE PRIMARY UNDERLYING FEELINGS

There is another group of secondary emotions that is desirable—the GLAD emotions. When we are pleased, comfortable, or experience any of the other GLAD emotions, we feel one or more of the pleasant underlying primary feelings—we feel WORTHY, ACCEPTABLE, or CAPABLE, or some combination of them. We call these the three WAC™ feelings.

> Emotional state:
>
>   If I am GLAD ...
>
> WAC underlying primary feelings:
>
>   ... I feel WORTHY, ACCEPTABLE, or CAPABLE.

Often, we feel all three of these primary feelings at the same time. Let's refer back to the story of Cindy and Dev. When they came up with the solution to their problem, this resulted in GLAD secondary emotions for Dev because he knew he had been heard, understood, and accepted. In addition, he felt WORTHY, ACCEPTABLE to himself, and quite CAPABLE. Cindy also had these feelings. The WAC feelings all occurred simultaneously.

Some time ago, a small group of adults recovering from drug abuse discussed these AGRUP and WAC feelings. Out of the blue, one of them exclaimed:

> "Oh, now I get it. Whenever I am out of WAC, I feel AGRUP!"

He was right. Even in everyday activities such as eating an apple, looking up at the sky, or reading a book, we often feel WORTHY, ACCEPTABLE, and CAPABLE. However, if we start to worry about something, all of a sudden, our WAC feelings vanish and we start to feel ACCUSED, GUILTY, REJECTED, UNLOVABLE, POWERLESS, or some combination of these feelings. This can occur completely within our minds without any outside influence.

RECOGNIZE HOW UNDERLYING PRIMARY FEELINGS IMPACT OUR CORE BELIEFS

The chart on the next page summarizes how our AGRUP and WAC feelings create our MAD, SAD, ANXIOUS, or GLAD emotions. For instance, when we are frustrated because we are caught in traffic, exasperation is often created because we feel POWERLESS. In addition, the chart illustrates how these feelings can also reinforce our Negative Core Beliefs. If the traffic is going to make us late to a meeting, we might think, "I am always late because I never plan enough time to get where I need to go. What an idiot I am."

By contrast, we can take a different perspective and become calm—a GLAD emotion. We might soothe ourselves by taking a few deep breaths and thinking, "This traffic is just a delay." By reassuring ourselves, we feel more WORTHY, ACCEPTABLE, and CAPABLE. We also strengthen our Positive Core Beliefs. Because we are concerned about being late, this might indicate that "I am thoughtful."

In other words, when I am MAD, SAD, or ANXIOUS, it is because I feel AGRUP, but this in turn reinforces one or more of my Negative Core Beliefs. However, when I am GLAD, it is because I feel WAC, which reinforces one or more of my Positive Core Beliefs.

See the chart on the next page for an illustration of these concepts.

UNDERLYING PRIMARY FEELINGS CREATE OUR EMOTIONS AND CONTRIBUTE TO OUR CORE BELIEFS

When I am MAD, SAD, or ANXIOUS ...

However, when I am GLAD ...

... it is because I feel:

ACCUSED

GUILTY

REJECTED

UNLOVABLE

POWERLESS

... it is because I feel:

WORTHY

ACCEPTABLE

CAPABLE

The above feelings
reinforce
Negative Core Beliefs,
such as:

"I am not good enough."

"I am stupid."

"I don't belong."

"I am a failure."

"I am unworthy to be loved."

The above feelings
reinforce
Positive Core Beliefs,
such as:

"I am good enough."

"I am intelligent."

"I am a good friend."

"I am succeeding."

"I am worthy to be loved."

As the chart shows, our AGRUP feelings strengthen our Negative Core Beliefs. These feelings provide evidence for our beliefs. For example, if we often feel ACCUSED, we might believe, "I am not good enough" or "There is something wrong with me." If we frequently feel POWERLESS it would be natural to believe, "I am helpless" or "I am weak." However, we do not have to accept these incorrect self-beliefs.

By contrast, the WAC feelings support Positive Core Beliefs. When we feel WORTHY, ACCEPTABLE, and CAPABLE, then we believe, "I am worthwhile, I am enough, and I am competent," or some other similar beliefs. These desirable feelings also create a greater degree of resilience when we encounter difficult or overwhelming experiences in the future.

In summary, our primary underlying feelings create our secondary emotions. At the same time, they reinforce either Positive or Negative Core Beliefs.

TRANSFORM AGRUP EXPERIENCES INTO POSITIVE CORE BELIEFS

We can learn from an upsetting experience by becoming aware of our feelings and changing them. For example, if we get into an argument with a friend and feel rejected and powerless, instead of staying upset, we can alter our feelings if:

❑   We recognize our MAD, SAD, or ANXIOUS emotions (e.g., "I'm frustrated because my friend disagrees with me") and become aware of the underlying primary feelings (e.g., "I definitely feel REJECTED and POWERLESS").

❑   We transform our feelings by creating a constructive action (e.g., "I need to hear what she is saying and try to understand her side of the story").

As we become aware of our MAD, SAD, or ANXIOUS emotions, we can also recognize our underlying primary feelings. It is then possible to exchange these feelings to feel WORTHY, ACCEPTABLE, or CAPABLE by thinking of an action that will be beneficial. In this way, we strengthen our positive belief, "I am competent."

We all have done this many times. For example, if Aunt Sally criticized something we said, we might think, "I am upset because of her criticism. I feel ACCUSED and a little REJECTED. However, Aunt Sally is having a bad day and I love her. I wonder what I can do to cheer her up." Instead of getting upset when we feel AGRUP, we can create more productive interactions. Learning how to consistently convert unfavorable situations into beneficial outcomes will bolster our Positive Core Beliefs.

DISCOVER HOW TO REGULATE EMOTIONS BY SOOTHING SELF-CARE AND POSITIVE ENGAGEMENT

We can learn to manage anger, sadness, and anxiousness through soothing self-care or constructively interacting with others. One day a woman said to her husband, "Rick, the trash was not put out to be picked up." Since Rick had agreed to set out the trash each Monday night, he felt ACCUSED, GUILTY, REJECTED, UNLOVABLE, and POWERLESS. He could have gotten MAD, SAD, or ANXIOUS about this, but he decided to handle the situation more positively.

Believe it or not, in handling all of the circumstances of our lives, we have only six possible choices. These four are unhelpful reactions to upsetting experiences:

❑   FIGHT OR ATTACK. Whenever we feel threatened, one reaction is strike out. Whether we face physical or emotional harm, many people naturally want to fight back. An argument is an example of a fight or attack reaction. For instance, Rick could have said something sarcastic or dismissive but he didn't.

❑   FLIGHT OR AVOID. When reacting to a threat, another option is to run. When we flee from a physical or an emotional assault, we are trying to ensure our safety. Leaving a party to escape talking with someone we don't like is an example of a flight or avoid reaction. Rick might have ignored the situation and pretended that he didn't hear what his wife had said, but he knew this would have been totally ineffectual.

❑   FREEZE OR NUMB. One way to deal with a danger is to shut down and do nothing. In a physical attack, we can become immobile. Sometimes we deaden psychological discomfort with drugs, video games, or other problematic behaviors. If Rick had decided to turn on a ball game, he would have been trying to numb out the problem.

❑ ATTACK SELF. This fourth reaction is used to reprimand ourselves. It is often used to deflect another person's verbal attack or our own self-accusation. We believe we are wrong so we beat ourselves up. Rick could have just told himself, "I am such an idiot. I can't even remember to take out the garbage."

In a few situations, the above four reactions may be somewhat valid ways to deal with physically or emotionally threatening conditions. However, in almost all psychologically menacing circumstances when we are MAD or ANXIOUS, these reactions are useless.

It is usually much more effective to choose one or both of the following helpful responses. This is what Rick chose to do:

❑ SOOTHING SELF-CARE. When we consciously choose to engage in soothing self-care, we have an increased ability to more effectively manage emotionally problematic situations. We do this by going for walks, meditating or praying, taking breaks for relaxation or recreation, or doing any other enjoyable personal activities. These soothing self-care opportunities are vital to our mental and emotional well-being.

Instead of getting defensive, Rick calmed down by taking a couple of deep breaths. These deep breaths provided a measure of self-care. He then recognized that he was not fulfilling his responsibility to take out the garbage.

❑ CONSTRUCTIVE INTERACTION. Constructively interacting with others is the only other positive response that can be chosen to deal with difficult interpersonal problems. Instead of one of the four undesirable reactions, we can make the conscious choice to respond in a caring and productive way.

After a brief pause to gather his thoughts, Rick said to his wife, "You're right. This isn't the first time. I am going to figure out a way to remember to take out the trash each Monday. He knew he could devise a plan to do better. By constructively interacting with his wife, he not only confirmed to his wife that she was important to him, he also strengthened their connection with each other.

Rick's plan was to put a sticky note on his mirror in the bathroom. Twice a day, for seven days, he saw that note. The next Monday, he remembered to take out the trash and never forgot it again. Not only had he created an effective reminder, he had also created a constructive interaction with his partner. He felt pretty good about himself. Unsurprisingly, this strengthened his three WAC self-beliefs, "I am WORTHY, I am ACCEPTABLE, and I am CAPABLE."

Soothing self-care effectively calms and regulates our emotions. Instead of resorting to fight, flight, freeze, or attacking ourselves, we can use a variety of means to reduce our anxiety, anger, and sadness. Then, we are able to think more clearly and we are much more likely to create better solutions.

Constructive interaction with others effectively creates stronger interpersonal connections, greater cooperation, and more favorable outcomes. We reinforce our Positive Core Beliefs as we demonstrate to ourselves that we are, in word and behavior, WORTHY, ACCEPTABLE, and CAPABLE. These are three of our most productive Key Core Beliefs.

OTHER IMPORTANT EMOTIONAL SKILLS TO CONSIDER

In the first part of this chapter, we focused on understanding our underlying feelings, our secondary emotions, and the measures we can take to regulate our emotional experiences. By more effectively regulating our emotions and by learning soothing self-care and constructive interaction, we grow in our capacity to be ever more successful.

These are skills of emotional self-regulation. They have helped many individuals overcome devastating difficulties and highly disturbing interactions with others.

For the remainder of this chapter, we will review other important emotional skills we can use as valuable tools in managing our lives, including:

❑   The skill of realistic and positive self-assessing

❑   The skill of taking responsibility

❑   The skill of describing behaviors instead of applying labels

❑   The skill of exercising empathy

❑   The skill of appreciating each person

❑   The skill of creating our mutual best interests

❑   The skill of deeply connecting

As we review these emotional skills, consider which of these skills might be the most valuable for your self-growth. By focusing on the improvement of one or more emotional skills, our awareness will grow and we will strengthen our Positive Core Beliefs as well as our Self-Belief Identity.

THE SKILL OF REALISTIC AND POSITIVE SELF-ASSESSING

It is possible and worthwhile for all of us to evaluate both our strengths and limitations. Doing this makes it more likely that we will learn how to better use our abilities while we simultaneously work on our shortcomings.

When we perceive ourselves realistically, we see a whole person. Of course, we all have some limitations. If a person is small in height and does not have excellent hand-eye coordination, it is highly unlikely that he or she will ever play sports professionally. Also, everyone makes mistakes. We can learn from slip-ups whether they are our responsibility or not our fault.

The mistakes we make give us the opportunity to grow and develop as individuals. When we observe a young child learning to walk, and frequently tripping and falling we recognize he or she is going through a learning process. No one criticizes a child for stumbling while mastering the complicated skills of balance and motor coordination. Likewise, self-blame or getting down on ourselves when we make a mistake is not helpful. Self-criticism, and the criticism of others, is of little to no value. Even so-called constructive criticism usually feels like disapproval. Obviously, in order to learn, we often need feedback. Sincere, helpful feedback is valuable and beneficial.

Learning to perceive our whole self requires focusing less on our shortcomings and more on our positive qualities. As we have discussed, it is amazing that when individuals are asked to list 10 positive characteristics and 10 negative characteristics, most can quickly identify the negatives but take much longer to come up with the positives. This is especially interesting because nearly everyone has many more favorable qualities than undesirable ones.

Consider taking a few minutes to list as many of your positive qualities as you can. Post these qualities where you will see them every day. Add to your list whenever you think of a new one. Don't worry about your shortcomings—you already know them. Focus on realistically seeing your positive self.

THE SKILL OF TAKING RESPONSIBILITY

Once we make a decision, we need to be accountable for it. If the decision does not work out, we can always devise another option. Unfortunately, many of us do not fully appreciate the power of owning the complete responsibility for our emotions, thoughts, and actions.

It's probably safe to say that each of us has occasionally avoided personal accountability in order to avoid unpleasant consequences. It seems to be an almost universal human trait. One of the ways to avoid being personally accountable is to blame others. But when we minimize or deny our responsibility and then throw another person "under the bus," we weaken ourselves.

Conversely, when we are fully responsible, we understand the freedom associated with our accountability and we own our lives. We don't have to look over our shoulders and we don't play games with others. If we have distressed others, we apologize and make amends. We know we are reliable and others can trust us. When we have this degree of integrity, we are authentic, honest, and confident. Therefore, we act with greater self-assurance. There is real power in being responsible.

THE SKILL OF DESCRIBING BEHAVIORS INSTEAD OF APPLYING LABELS

Labels are used every day to demean and belittle others. It is amazing how easy it is to say things such as, "He is such a jerk," "I can't stand that liar," "She is really a snob, isn't she?" "I never met a bigger idiot," and "He is a first-class klutz." Labels are cheap ways to wrongly describe other individuals. It takes very little intelligence to label.

Those who are emotionally self-aware strive never to label people. When we are mindful of how hurtful they are, we have no need to label others. Instead of labeling the person, we can accurately describe their behavior. For example, instead of saying, "He is so mean," we can say, "Sometimes, he acts meanly."

One of the primary advantages of not using labels is rarely appreciated—people who refuse to label others seldom label themselves. For example, if we refuse to call anyone a jerk, we will be much less likely to label ourselves as a jerk. By contrast, when we unfavorably label ourselves, we always reinforce disagreeable and mistaken Negative Core Beliefs. By not labeling others with sarcastic or scornful descriptions, we avoid falling into the trap of creating scornful descriptions of ourselves.

THE SKILL OF EXERCISING EMPATHY

Chapter 6 made the case for the crucial importance of empathy. By exercising empathy, we more fully understand others, their thoughts, and their feelings.

We want to emphasize that empathy is our most decisive interpersonal skill and offers the greatest advantages. The ability to empathize is inherent in each of us. However, it is a skill that can be finely tuned by consistently practicing how to use our understanding of others. For instance, in most conversations, we listen to others for primarily one of two reasons:

We listen so we can say something in return based on our own experiences, or

We listen to learn and to better understand the other person.

During any conversation, in the background of our minds is a constant self-discussion. This self-talk concentrates on either what we are next going to say in reply (e.g., "It sounds like he had a great vacation, but wait until I tell him what I did!"), or it centers on our interest in the other person (e.g., "His vacation sounds interesting. I want to know more about what he did").

Three characteristics are associated with empathy. For instance, if someone is telling us about a recent rock-climbing adventure, we want them to know that we hear them, that we are trying to understand them, and that we accept them without judgment.

❑   HEAR. As we use empathy, we assure the other person we are paying attention to the content of what is being said to us (e.g., "Based on what you said, it seems like the manager was not listening to you—tell me more.").

❑   UNDERSTAND. When we do our best to be empathetic, we also attempt to understand the other person's emotions (e.g., "It seems like that was really frustrating—how did it feel?").

❑   ACCEPT. We don't have to agree with the other person but we listen without judgment or criticism and with an open mind and heart (e.g., "I don't know what I would have done, but it sounds like you did the best you could").

When we have been heard, understood, and accepted—we feel valued. (Recall "Dev's Story" earlier in this chapter.)

As a child, many of us had wonderful grandparents who took the time to hear our childlike, mundane tales. We knew that they wanted to understand us and we felt understood. Also, they accepted us without criticism. Needless to say, we loved to share our experiences with them.

By becoming more skilled in using empathy, we naturally increase our Positive Core Beliefs. We believe: "I am caring because I really listen to others. I am understanding. I am accepting of others without judgment."

THE SKILL OF APPRECIATING EACH PERSON

We can grow to appreciate each person we meet. The word appreciate has two related meanings. Most commonly it means to be grateful. However, it also means to value. To illustrate this, in real estate—if a property appreciates—it increases in worth.

Everyone is of equal worth. For example, if we brought together a hundred infants from around the world, none of these babies would have more or less value than any of the others. Each of them would deserve to be treated with human dignity and respect. Irrespective of any differences, there is no reason to assume one child would have greater worth than another.

Just as this is true of children, it is also true for each of us. If we had a group of a hundred individuals from as many different countries, none would have more inherent value than any of the others. Each person has basic worth as a human. Everyone has different strengths and limitations, but we cannot say one individual is fundamentally less valuable.

As adults, when we respect others, we value them and allow them to make their own decisions. We give them the same measure of respect that we want for ourselves. We do not have to agree with their choices or go along with what they have decided. We can be assertive without being either impassive or antagonistic.

To truly appreciate others, we acknowledge their inherent human dignity. When we do this, everyone has our respect regardless of their age, nationality, gender, orientation, race, language, family wealth, or any other factor. As we come to truly believe each person is worthy of human dignity, our respect for ourselves similarly increases.

When we value others as well as ourselves, we are freed from comparing ourselves to others. We no longer have the need for judgments. If we see someone with exceptional intellectual capabilities, we do not say, "I am not as smart as she is." Instead, we might simply say, "She is such a quick learner." We can recognize another person's unique abilities without diminishing our own. Likewise, when we encounter a person who has achieved less than we have, we have no need to think, "Compared to him, I am more successful."

No one has more or less human dignity. Although our circumstances are varied, we are linked to every other person because we share both our humanity and our mortality. When we develop our emotional skills, we will be much more likely to appreciate the human dignity and worth of everyone else. We will also increase other Positive Core Beliefs such as, "I am valuable" and "I am appreciative."

THE SKILL OF CREATING OUR MUTUAL BEST INTERESTS

When we get what we want at the expense of others' interests, the outcomes are rarely, if ever, satisfying. We all know what it feels like when someone takes advantage of us, overlooks our desires, or dismisses what is important to us. Almost always this results in a poor outcome. The aftermath of being on the losing side engenders feelings of resentment. If this happens repeatedly, the relationship deteriorates. Many friendships—as well as family relationships—end when the desire to win becomes more important than agreeing to create solutions that are in everyone's best interests.

Approaching problems with the concept of "our mutual best interests" (see Chapter 6) will enable us to work with others to achieve truly effective outcomes. We do this by proposing jointly valuable solutions to problems. This requires employing empathy to come up with outcomes that benefit others as well as ourselves. As we practice teamwork, cooperation, conflict resolution, and negoti-ation, we also increase our Positive Core Beliefs such as, "I am a team player," "I am a problem-solver," and "I am open to others' ideas."

Creating solutions that are in everyone's best interest takes some time and effort. But the results work, and we feel better about who we are and also about our relationships. When we team up with a family member, someone at work, or members of our sports team, we cannot help but sense an increase in our own worth and in the worth of others.

THE SKILL OF DEEPLY CONNECTING

Each of us began our lives with a strong connection to our mothers. Since then, we have continually tried to connect with others. Our success as an individual always depends on other people. Of course, we need to be self-reliant and responsible when it is appropriate. However, when we fail to deeply and caringly connect with others, we begin to isolate ourselves.

One of the most common aspects of mental and emotional illness occurs when a person disconnects from others and believes that he or she is alone. A person may think, "No one understands me." "No one cares." "My experience is unique." "No one likes me." These thoughts relate to the formation or reinforcement of a number of other Negative Core Beliefs such as, "I am insignificant and I don't matter." Many similar beliefs create a sense of separation that is directly linked to depression and anxiety. Serious mental concerns such as self-harm, drug or behavioral addictions, clinical depression, post-traumatic stress, and most other disorders share this sense of isolation from others.

By contrast, when we feel connected to others, we live more fulfilling and enjoyable lives. People who actively engage in club activities, exercise groups, religious communities, work groups, sports teams, community service initiatives, professional associations, hobby groups, and many other types of activities report a greater measure of life satisfaction and added happiness.

Additionally, in countless small ways, we can strengthen our ability to foster caring connections. One person who considered improving her association with others tried an experiment. Each day, she focused on consciously connecting with others by smiling 10 times. After a week, she noticed that she felt better about herself so she decided to continue the experiment and soon discovered that she became more positive with all of her relationships. She said that this was particularly true in her connection to her partner.

Not coincidentally, these individuals also develop greater resistance to both physical health problems and psychological concerns. Part of a good recipe for wellness and well-being is to promote the skill of developing positive, empathetic, and mutually beneficial relationships. When we constructively engage with others, we measurably add to our HEART Health Integration (the five

HEART essentials are HEALTH, EMOTIONS, AWARENESS, RELATIONSHIPS, and TRANSCENDENCE, discussed in Chapter 2). One of the most powerful building blocks of our crucial Key Core Beliefs is, "I am deeply connected."

All of the emotional skills can enrich the quality of our relationships and greatly enhance our Self-Belief Identity. In becoming more aware of these skills and in more fully developing them, we learn how to more meaningfully tell the story of our lives.

WRITING THE STORY OF OUR LIFE

Sometimes it seems extremely difficult to change one's Negative Core Beliefs, but a strong rationale exists for doing so. Orlando was talking with a friend about his unhappy cousin, Lionel. After recovering from dependence on alcohol 15 years ago, Lionel still faced a number of problems. He was unable to maintain close relationships and he always seemed to be depressed, unwanted, and unneeded.

LIONEL'S STORY

Despite his recovery from alcoholism, it was clear that Lionel had never addressed his strongly held Negative Core Beliefs. Many of his worst self-beliefs stemmed from his childhood. Lionel's father had physically and emotionally abused him, and his mother had emotionally mistreated him. He worked his entire life to gain the approval of others but ended up in fruitless relationships that triggered his need to drink and escape reality. Somehow, he seemed to be a magnet for abusive people.

Lionel's life was dreadful and he never had a supportive family environment. He was constantly at risk of a drinking relapse. When he was encouraged to change his Negative Core Beliefs, Lionel dismissed this and said, "There is no way that I am ever going to fix the mess I am in now."

He was in this mess because his Negative Core Beliefs projected a mindset that attracted individuals who wanted to dominate and belittle him. He could stop being a magnet for these emotionally abusive people if he developed consistent Positive Core Beliefs. This would be the vital first step for him to attract healthier and more supportive people into his life.

With the encouragement of Orlando, Lionel realized that he could change his Negative Core Beliefs. Once he experimented with this, he found a great deal of personal satisfaction in seeing himself both realistically and positively. It took some determined effort on his part but he would not give up. After years of battling depression, he was amazed to discover he could finally start to write the story of who he really wanted to be.

Like Lionel, all of us are writing the story of our life. If we resist changing our Negative Core Beliefs, we lose the opportunity of living better lives. However, when we choose to cultivate healthy beliefs, we naturally draw others to us who have similar favorable self-beliefs. They will help us enrich our lives and we will begin to be more supportive of them. Only then, can we write the story we want for ourselves.

Each day we create a page for our life's story. As we develop emotional skills, we can regularly assess how we are doing. One way to do this is to daily review our lives as illustrated on the chart below.

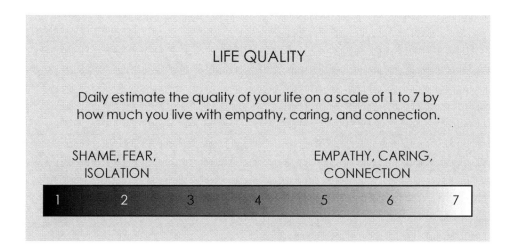

LIFE QUALITY

Daily estimate the quality of your life on a scale of 1 to 7 by how much you live with empathy, caring, and connection.

SHAME, FEAR, ISOLATION				EMPATHY, CARING, CONNECTION		
1	2	3	4	5	6	7

We all constantly live on the scale of Life Quality. When we continually cultivate our Positive Core Beliefs, we strengthen our abilities to be empathetic, caring, and connected. Every so often, we may feel some shame, fear, or isolation. This is part of the human experience that we share with every other person. Nevertheless, we also have the capability to move from shame to empathy, from fear to caring, and from isolation to connection.

This shift often occurs quite naturally. Let's say we get annoyed with someone we care about. In most situations, we will resolve our annoyance and will again enjoy our relationship. As we make conscientious efforts to do this, sooner rather than later, our emotional skills develop more fully. We become more proficient at becoming self-aware and in moving from a "2" or "3" on the scale to a "6" or "7."

The term "imagineer" is a combination of the words "imagine" and "engineer." Walt Disney popularized this concept as he encouraged others to combine their ingenuity and vision together with their ability to plan and develop. In a real sense, we all are using our imagination to engineer every day of our lives. By practicing our emotional skills, we are writing our story and becoming more skilled in empathy, taking responsibility, valuing others, and staying connected.

As we build our emotional skills, we will imagineer the story we want to write. Regardless of challenges, concerns, or achievements—it will be our story and we will be proud of it. Along the way, our Positive Core Beliefs will result in a more resilient Self-Belief Identity. Our HEART essentials will improve and our Core-Related Health will measurably increase.

REVIEW ACTIVITY
Chapter 8

Take a few minutes to review the emotional skills described in this chapter. Which of these skills would be the most important for you to improve?

What could you do to develop one or more of the emotional skills?

Daily, what would you do to increase these skills?

How would you specifically measure your progress?

Would it worthwhile to ask for support and feedback from someone you trust?

You can print out each Chapter Review Activity under the Activities tab at
KeyCoreBeliefs.org. At the end of most of the Chapter Review Activities,
you'll find a link to additional activities that are available without cost.

NOTES: What other ideas do you have concerning the emotional skills reviewed in this chapter?

Section Three

ELEVATING OUR KEY CORE BELIEFS

PRINCIPLE HARMONY

Matching Our Behaviors to Our Values

Things do not change. We change.

Henry David Thoreau

HOW CAN ALIGNING OUR ACTIONS WITH OUR VALUES INCREASE POSITIVE CORE BELIEFS?

One of the most overlooked contributing factors to mental and emotional illness is the misalignment of behaviors and values. For example, if a person believes honesty is an important value and yet is not consistently honest with others, that individual will experience an inner conflict. The conflict will increase his or her level of anxiety and influence his or her Negative Core Beliefs.

A value is defined as a principle, standard, or quality that is considered personally worthwhile or desirable. Our values are generally associated with what we consider to be right or wrong. We individually select our values because we believe they will help us make suitable and beneficial choices. These choices typically work for us as well as others.

Each of us has selected a large number of values. However, it is ultimately up to us to determine how we will be guided in choosing our values and whether they will be in agreement with how we act. Every day, we choose to live either in harmony or out of harmony with our values. Malia's story demonstrates how past experiences and our Key Core Beliefs relate to our values and the choices we make.

MALIA'S STORY

Malia had been through two divorces and a recent devastating breakup with a boyfriend. She could not understand how these relationships had been so disastrous, so she made an appointment with Gretchen, a mental health professional. In counseling, Malia learned that the abuse she had suffered as a child could have had a significant influence on her adult relationships. When Gretchen asked Malia to see if she noticed any patterns, Malia noted two things that had occurred in her previous relationships.

First, she said that all three of her former partners had been abusive. Her first husband was physically abusive and this resulted in domestic violence charges and their divorce. Both of her other relationships had been emotionally abusive. When Malia had stood up for herself, the second husband began an affair, which resulted in the second divorce. In her last relationship, when she refused to be intimidated by the emotional manipulation of her boyfriend, he immediately broke up with her.

Second, Malia noted that in each of these three relationships, she had gambled with her partners. In fact, her first husband had introduced her to gambling. She met her second husband and her boyfriend in casinos. Although she liked the excitement of gambling, she hated to lose. Malia had grown up in a modest home without a lot of money. Regardless of the fun and excitement of gambling, it bothered her that she was throwing away her hard-earned cash. She said, "Sometimes it feels like I'm lighting a match to my paycheck."

When Gretchen asked about Malia's childhood, she recounted being sexually abused from when she was 4 until she was 9 by a sibling who was five years older. The abuse finally came to an end when her father caught them in her bedroom. Malia and her brother were equally punished and both were accused of being "very bad." Out of this came a shame-based, Negative Core Belief, "If I am sexual, I am a bad person." From that time on, Malia did not engage in sex until she met her first husband.

As she discussed her childhood and the Negative Core Beliefs it resulted in with Gretchen, Malia identified two more Core Beliefs:

"I attract the wrong kind of men. I must be undeserving of love."

"There is something wrong with me because others abuse me."

Through diligent effort, Malia began to understand how both of these Negative Core Beliefs were untrue. She began to develop Positive Core Beliefs and this made it possible for her to perceive herself more realistically and positively. She also began to see how her childhood abuse had played a part in her adult relationships.

Based on her new understanding, Malia started to remember the harmful behaviors of each of her partners before the relationships became serious. As she worked with her counselor, she gained a heightened awareness of their totally inappropriate conduct. In the future, this would help her avoid undesirable relationships. Additionally, she realized how her past fear of losing the affection of others had worked against her. With more resilience, she became more confident in her ability to love and to be loved.

Along with a better knowledge of her fears, Malia realized that going to casinos had been exciting because she been able to let go of her sexual self-consciousness. In her mind, she felt free and desirable. However, this freedom came at a price, because then she felt she had to be compliant with the demands of her partners. If she did not agree to meet their sexual desires, she risked losing them.

Although Malia had been separated from her boyfriend for more than a year, every two weeks she still traveled to an out-of-town casino, which had cost her quite a bit of money. When asked whether she enjoyed these gambling excursions, she immediately replied, "No, I hate losing so much, but it's hard to pass up the excitement."

As soon as she said this, Malia recognized how she had disconnected herself from her own values. Somehow her gambling had been enmeshed in her sense of self-permission to spontaneously engage in uninhibited sex with her partners. Although not logical, her sexuality had been linked to the excitement of gambling. For the first time, she began to see how gambling had become an ineffective coping mechanism to suppress the past humiliation of her abusive partners. Even a year after her breakup, Malia was still trying to bury her Negative Core Beliefs through her trips to casinos.

When Malia learned how to resolve these related experiences, her casino trips stopped because she no longer had any desire to gamble. Her behaviors became more aligned with her values. In a few weeks, she developed the new Positive Core Beliefs, "I am deserving of respect" and "I am okay just as I am." No longer bound by her past, she began to build the future she really wanted. Several months later, she developed a wonderful friendship with a new coworker. This friend soon became a caring, respectful, and loving partner.

We should note that Malia's story is not about whether gambling is right or wrong. It is only about whether gambling was in harmony with her personal values. Indeed, in discussing "right and wrong," sometimes it is more helpful to ask instead, "What works or what doesn't work?" Our values should act as guides to show us how to make effective choices. Gambling simply did not work for Malia.

Of course, gambling doesn't work for anyone who has an addictive gambling habit or for those who have strong religious or cultural values regarding gaming. It also does not work when people bet money that should be used for the needs of their family or when potential losses would create financial problems. Obviously, where gambling is illegal, it is sensible to abide by the law.

Whether one drinks alcohol or not also serves as an example of values that guide our choices. Some people enjoy moderate drinking or having a drink with family or friends. Others have decided that drinking is problematic and does not work for them. Their value excludes alcohol because they view drinking as detrimental.

Other individuals refrain from drinking for a variety of personal reasons, such as a belief that "alcoholism runs in my family." Therefore, they never drink alcoholic beverages. Others believe that even social drinking can be unhealthy. Many people abstain from alcohol because they don't want to be impaired, or they don't want to risk driving while under the influence. Clearly, many explanations exist for choosing the value to refrain from even moderate alcohol consumption.

As previously discussed, drinking or using drugs as a coping mechanism is ineffective and damaging. All other negatively compulsive behaviors used to cope with distress are also ineffective. In the context of this discussion about values, harmful coping mechanisms simply cannot work. Most of us have a natural sense of any behavior that will cause problems for us. If we recognize a detrimental means of coping, we need to find alternative coping skills in harmony with our values. Soothing self-care activities, such as a hobby or positive interactions with good friends, are examples of effective coping skills.

Some compulsive coping behaviors require the support of mental health professionals to overcome. These may include alcohol or drug addictions, eating disorders, addictive gambling, or any other compulsive behavior. Effective treatment includes dealing with the related Negative Core Beliefs that always contribute to the addiction.

VALUES ARE CRUCIAL TO OUR KEY CORE BELIEFS

We all have a number of principal values that are decisive to how we think and behave. They serve as a personal compass. These values are linked to one or more of our Positive Core Beliefs that are also values:

- ❑ "I am honest."
- ❑ "I am reliable."
- ❑ "I am hard-working."
- ❑ "I am frugal."
- ❑ "I am respectful."
- ❑ "I am kind."

However, when our behaviors do not line up with our principal values, we become detached from our own standards of conduct and our Key Core Beliefs become compromised. This creates inner emotional conflicts. We can try to suppress these internal conflicts, or we can consciously choose to disregard our values. Both choices inevitably lead to contradictory and confusing behaviors. If individuals consistently act contrary to their own standards of behavior, over time their values will be undermined. In addition, Negative Core Beliefs will be reinforced. For instance:

- ❑ If the value is honesty, repeated dishonesty can create the Negative Core Belief, "I am deceitful."

- ❑ If the value is reliability, inconsistent behaviors could result in the Negative Core Belief, "I am unreliable."

- ❑ If the value is hard work, slacking off can become the Negative Core Belief, "I am lazy."

- ❑ If the value is prudence, wasteful actions may result in the Negative Core Belief, "I am careless."

- ❑ If the value is to be respectful, repeated disrespect towards others could become the Negative Core Belief, "I am selfish."

- ❑ If the value is kindness, callous conduct may lead to the Negative Core Belief, "I am thoughtless."

Problems arise when we try to disregard our values. Our perceptions and emotions become distorted, and this can confuse our thinking and our choices. We put a lot at risk when we ignore our values. When we behave badly, we might minimize what we did, blame others, change the subject, bring up old hurts, start arguing, become sullen, or engage in some other questionable behavior, all of which cause increased inner anxiety. For example, if we are dishonest, we will have to watch what we say in the future so that we will not be caught in our lie.

Typically, our relationships also suffer. For instance, many quarrels occur when one partner is trying to hide something and the other person asks a question that is taken the wrong way. This creates anxiousness for the deceptive partner. Anger flares, reason disappears, and then we wind up in a pointless argument. Every day, we need to decide whether we will live in conflict with ourselves or select a path of internal harmony.

RESOLVING THE CONFLICTS BETWEEN OUR VALUES AND ACTIONS

By far, the best way to overcome any conflicts between our values and actions is to focus on changing how we choose to behave. All of us occasionally become disconnected from our personal standards of conduct. For example, we may usually be a caring person but after a long day of work, we might find ourselves snapping at our partner. In this situation, all we have to do is sincerely apologize—without excusing our behavior—and then resume being kind and considerate.

However, we may need a more focused effort for problem behaviors that are deep-rooted. This usually involves:

1.   Identifying the personal values that we want to concentrate on,

2.   Recognizing any past behaviors that don't match these values,

3.   Planning steps to correct the badly chosen behaviors as soon as we can, and

4.   Taking the necessary corrective actions and making amends if that is appropriate.

Let's explore how this might work. For instance, if honesty is a problem, we need to identify and fully understand our values regarding trustworthiness. We might ask ourselves, "How truthful do I really want to be?" It might seem like a silly question, but we need to be completely honest with ourselves. We need to decide when we will be fully honest or when it will be okay to "fudge the truth a little."

This raises the question of white lies. For example, when our partner asks us, "Honestly, how does this make me look?" Rather than the brutal truth, we might opt for gentle honesty by saying, "I think the blue one looks better, but if you like what you have chosen, you should wear it." This would be truthful and trustworthy.

Also, we need to know just how honest we will be when we are confronted with the need to be trustworthy. It may be helpful to actually write down a statement such as

> "I need to be honest with my partner at all times. I will not deceive her
> or leave out important information."

Identifying the degree of our honesty is an important first step. Only then can we recognize when our behavior is not in harmony with our values. For example, we might recall an event when we were not completely truthful.

> "I remember when I didn't tell my partner about all the money I spent
> on my sports equipment. When she confronted me,
> I lied about the actual amount and then immediately brought up
> all the money she has spent. When I think about it,
> I have done this more than a few times."

When we acknowledge our past actions, we learn how to be more conscious of what we have done. This often highlights any pattern of similar actions. By increasing the awareness of our behavioral patterns, we understand when our actions have not aligned with our values.

Then, we can devise a plan to harmonize our behaviors. For example,

> "In the future, if I say something untruthful, I am going to admit it.
> It probably will not go over well, but I want her to know
> she can rely on me to be honest."

By making a plan, we create a neurological link in our brain. This link makes it more likely that we will recognize any future problematic thinking or behavior and will make an appropriate correction. For example, this individual might determine,

> "In the future, if I am dishonest, I will tell my partner
> I have not been completely honest and I will make amends
> by doing something she likes to do. I could turn off the computer and
> spend some time with her such as going for a walk."

Making amends does not have to be a giant sacrifice. However, it does have to be sincere and it also has to be an action of value to the person who was hurt. If this occurred, she would be able to more fully trust her partner. Assuming the honesty remained consistent over time, the outcome would be positive for both of them.

Although this example focused on being honest, the same approach could be used to correct any patterns of action that have become problematic. Regardless of the past, old behaviors can be changed.

VALUES SUPPORT KEY CORE BELIEFS, SELF-BELIEF IDENTITY, AND HEALTH INTEGRATION

Aligning our values with our behaviors strengthens Positive Core Beliefs such as, "I am responsible." This decreases any previous anxiety that took place when our actions were not in keeping with our values. The results can be remarkable.

Relationship benefits will naturally occur, including mutual respect, enhanced empathy, and connection. These benefits combine to increase a stronger Self-Belief Identity. When values and behaviors are in harmony, we feel a greater measure of peace and genuine self-assurance, and an increased degree of mental and emotional well-being. By consistently aligning our values with our actions, we also cultivate the five essentials of HEART (HEALTH, EMOTIONS, AWARENESS, RELATIONSHIPS, and TRANSCENDENCE). Anxiety decreases, awareness improves, relationships become more connected, and all of this promotes overall Core-Related Health.

REVIEW ACTIVITY
Chapter 9

Here are a few questions worth considering.

Identify 10 of your important values. Take a few minutes to write them down.

1.

2.

3.

4.

5.

6.

7.

8.

9.

10.

Are any of these personal values not aligned with your behaviors? Most of us have one or more behaviors that are not fully in line with our values.

What can you do to recognize when your behaviors do not match your values? Becoming more aware of behaviors that are not in keeping with your own standards can help you change the patterns of your actions.

When you become aware of a mismatch between your values and behaviors, what can you do to change the behavior effectively? For example, when you perceive you are putting a spin on something you did, you could say something like, "Let me rephrase this so you have a more complete understanding of what happened."

You can print out each Chapter Review Activity under the Activities tab at KeyCoreBeliefs.org. At the end of most of the Chapter Review Activities, you'll find a link to additional activities that are available without cost.

NOTES: What impressions do you have about the discussion in this chapter about your personal values and how they influence your Key Core Beliefs?

CHAPTER 10

GREAT PARTNERSHIPS

The Prospects for Cooperative Success

*Never let a problem to be solved become
more important than a person to be loved.*

Thomas S. Monson

HOW CAN BUILDING RELATIONSHIPS ENRICH OUR MOST POSITIVE CORE BELIEFS?

As we discussed in Chapter 3, our Key Core Beliefs come into existence primarily through our interactions with others. The process of developing these beliefs started to form at birth and we continue to create, modify, or transform self-beliefs throughout our lives.

In our first few years, each of us had limited opportunities to change the nature of our interactions with others. We grew up as infants among adults who seemed to control all aspects of our lives, and we were totally dependent on our caregivers. As we gained more capabilities throughout childhood, we began to perceive ourselves differently. At some point, we started to form relationships with individuals who were not family members. These friendships were an important and crucial part of our development.

When we were teens, we wanted more freedom and more independence from our parents. After a few years, most of us also begin to experience a desire for a committed relationship and we started to search for a partner with whom we could deeply connect. As we have noted, all of our experiences with others are intricately intertwined with our most fundamental self-beliefs. We believe either

"I am worthy to be loved,"

or

"I am unworthy to be loved."

For each of us, one of these Key Core Beliefs prevails. Whichever belief dominates, it greatly shapes every facet of our lives. Many of us do not fully understand which belief is foremost. However, it takes only a few minutes of self-examination to learn which of these two beliefs is predominant.

Denise's story illustrates this.

DENISE'S STORY

Denise, the oldest of three children, grew up in a caring family that included her parents and her maternal grandmother. She had a particularly wonderful relationship with her father. The family lived in a small apartment but they had enough to live comfortably.

When Denise was 11, her father was killed in an automobile accident. Everyone in the family was devastated, but Denise was especially shattered because she had been so close to him. Eventually, she worked through her grief and had an ordinary adolescent life. In high school, she was popular and in her junior year, she developed an intense relationship with a young man who was a year older. They dated exclusively for that year before he left for college in another state.

Their relationship did not last. When he told Denise that he was seeing someone else, she felt betrayed and abandoned. She felt as bad as when she grieved for her father and she hated it. Before long, she found another boyfriend but a few months later, this relationship also came to an end. After graduation, she had another serious relationship that she thought would lead to an engagement. Instead, he left her for one of her girlfriends. Denise could not understand why every time she became involved with a guy, he left her.

On the outside, Denise was a happy, well-adjusted person. However, on the inside she believed there had to be something wrong with her. Her mother noticed she was spending more and more time at work. Socially, she had only two girlfriends. This continued until Denise was approaching her 25th birthday.

Finally, her mother wanted to know what was going on. Feeling unhappy about turning 25, Denise opened up. She said, "I realize I'm never going to have a relationship like you had with Dad. Every guy I've dated has dumped me. Somehow, they all knew I wasn't worth getting into a serious relationship with. In fact, I don't even like guys anymore. Some guys ask me out but I always say, 'I'm too busy' because I'm just not interested. The only people I feel close to are my girlfriends." Then to reinforce her lack of a social life she added, "And you know what? Why should I bother with love and romance? It didn't exactly end in a 'happily ever after' for you and Dad, did it?"

Denise's mother was stunned. She had never suspected her charming, intelligent, and successful daughter harbored such devastating beliefs about herself. It was fortunate for Denise that her mom decided to focus on better understanding her daughter's concerns. After a number of conversations, it became clear that Denise was purposely shutting out any possibility of a committed, loving relationship.

Her mother had previously seen a mental health professional, Anna, who understood the power of Key Core Beliefs. This counselor had been instrumental in helping the family work through the death of Denise's father. Since then, her mother had continued to see her from time to time. As she better understood her daughter's situation, her mom asked Denise if Anna might be of help. Reluctantly, Denise agreed to meet with the counselor and this proved to be a turning point.

In the space of a few months, Denise learned about five qualities that changed how she interacted with others (you'll read about these "GREAT" qualities later in this chapter). She also grew to believe, "I am worthy to be loved!"

It is important to mention that no individual has to be in a romantic relationship in order to have a satisfying and worthwhile life; many people enjoy living on their own. But Denise was intentionally trying to avoid having relationships because she was afraid that she was unworthy of love. This belief was significantly influencing her other Key Core Beliefs and limiting the quality of her life.

Denise's story is not unusual. Indeed, at times most of us will feel insecure about our ability to have sustained, loving relationships. A wide variety of circumstances can create this uncertainty.

These include the self-doubts we had during our teenage years, the misgivings we had when any relationship came to an end, the problems and concerns that accompany a divorce, the many uncertainties that arise with the death of a loved one, the questions we have when we enter into any new relationship, and other problematic situations too numerous to list. All of these insecurities become magnified if we principally believe, "I am unworthy to be loved."

Additionally, most of us have some anxiousness regarding our current relationships. Perhaps we have worries about our interactions at work, problems with our friends, issues regarding our parents, concerns about our children, or questions about our partners. Friends can become upset, family members can be hurt, and work associations can become difficult. There always seems to be one or more relationships that we are worried about. It is almost as if we cannot escape the anxiety of our interpersonal concerns.

For mental health professionals who work with couples, it is quite common to hear someone say, "I just don't love him anymore" or "We fell out of love." Even couples who have had wonderful relationships for many years may start to think that they do not care for each other as much as they once did.

What happened to cause these concerns? In order to understand how this happens, we first have to understand the twofold nature of each relationship.

THE DUAL NATURE OF ALL RELATIONSHIPS

Every relationship actually consists of two relationships—our relationship with another person and that person's relationship with us. We may assume our experience is the same for both of us; however, this assumption is inaccurate and often leads to misunderstandings. Our perceptions, feelings, and thoughts are most often quite different from the other person's perceptions, feelings, and thoughts.

Research studies show that our experience with another person is never the same as their experience with us. A noted psychiatrist demonstrated this when he asked a patient to record her impressions of each counseling session immediately after she met with him. He did the same. His secretary compiled all of their notes but did not share them for some months. When, much later, he and his patient reviewed their notes, they were amazed at how differently they had experienced the sessions. What the psychiatrist had thought was important to his patient was often insignificant or had not even registered. The reverse was also true. His seemingly trivial comments had frequently proven to be vitally important.

In any shared event, we must accept that the event will be experienced quite differently by each person. When we grasp the dual nature of all relationships, we can better understand ourselves and more fully appreciate others.

FIVE QUALITIES OF COMMITTED RELATIONSHIPS

It is also vitally important to understand the meanings of friendship and love. For example, in counseling couples, some individuals have said they no longer love their partner. This prompts a question, "How do you know if you really love somebody?"

Jack and Beverly are a remarkable example of a devoted couple. They have been each other's best friend in a marriage that has lasted more than 50 years. Despite major illnesses and challenges, they both find delight in each other. They exemplify five key qualities of all caring relationships. Each quality can be phrased as a question that we ask ourselves:

1. Am I GENUINE? How much am I honest, sincere, open, and reliable so that others can completely trust me and be at ease with me?

2. Am I RESPECTFUL? How much do I honor the rights of others to make their own choices and to be responsible for their decisions even when I disagree with them?

3. Am I EMPATHETIC? How much do I care about others by really listening to them and striving to understand their emotions, fears, and desires?

4. Am I ACCEPTING? How much do I fully accept others as they are without imposing my expectations, values, judgments, or criticisms even if I differ with them?

5. Am I TRUSTFUL? How much do I believe in the good-hearted intentions of others by appreciating the best about them?

These five qualities of friendship are referred to by the acronym GREAT™. All wonderful relationships have a measurable degree of these qualities. Each quality is also a skill that we can develop.

CAN THE QUALITY OF A RELATIONSHIP BE MEASURED?

There is an old saying, "If you want to have a friend, be a friend." This is good advice. However, we can better define how to be a friend by paying attention to the five GREAT qualities. When we learn how to apply these skills more fully, we gain greater confidence and we form closer, more satisfying relationships. We also fortify highly valuable Positive Core Beliefs and strengthen our Self-Belief Identity.

In any circumstance, both individuals can assess how they would answer the above questions on a scale of 0 to 10. For example, Celeste has a friend, Isabelle. If Celeste is almost always honest, sincere, and reliable, she could rate her level of being GENUINE as "9." By contrast, if she was not at all GENUINE, she should rate that quality as "0."

Celeste is also very respectful that Isabelle can make her own decisions and be responsible for those decisions. She doesn't always agree with her friend's choices, but she always recognizes Isabelle's right to choose for herself, so she might rate RESPECTFUL as "10." In addition, Celeste tries to be empathetic by caring enough to really listen and understand Isabelle, so she might rate her level of being EMPATHETIC as "9." She can also assess herself on the other two scales of being ACCEPTING and TRUSTFUL. If her average score for all five qualities is "8.5," this would indicate to what extent Celeste is a good friend for Isabelle.

Isabelle could also rate herself on each of the five qualities. The average of Isabelle's scores might be "9" since it is common for two good friends to have nearly equal total scores. In fact, when any two people have a positive relationship with each other, their scores will often be quite close for each of the five GREAT qualities.

When the score is consistently "8" or above for each of the five qualities and for both individuals, their relationships with each other are mutually beneficial and enjoyable. Wonderful friendships, constructive working relations, and all other positive relationships always rest on the consistent application of these five qualities. This is especially true for committed partner relationships.

AN EXERCISE IN FRIENDSHIP MEASUREMENT

Each of us can gauge the GREAT qualities of any of our relationships. For example, think of someone with whom you have a strong friendship. It could be a sibling, a close friend, a grandparent, a friend at work, or anyone else you truly care about. Using the bar graph below, answer each of the questions on the next page by rating each quality on a scale of 0 to 10. In the bar graph, write the score you give yourself in each of the left columns below the qualities of GENUINE, RESPECTFUL, EMPATHETIC, ACCEPTING, and TRUSTFUL.

Now estimate how GENUINE the other person is with you. Believe it or not, we all have the ability to accurately assess another person's GREAT qualities if we have a fairly close relationship. Think of a score that person might give about his or her own qualities if you were doing the exercise together. After estimating his or her genuineness, mark the score in the bar on the right column in the first pair of bars below GENUINE in the graph. Then continue to estimate what the other person would give for his or her scores for RESPECTFUL, EMPATHETIC, ACCEPTING, and TRUSTFUL.

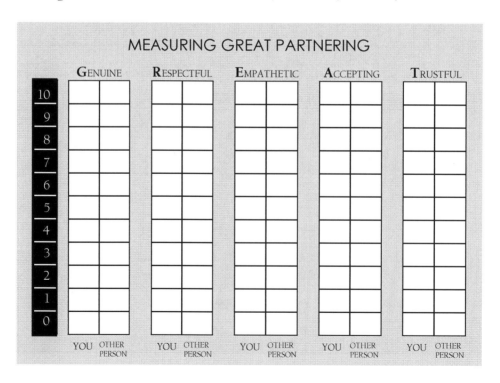

Here are the questions to answer to determine the scores for each of the five qualities of any relationship you have with another person:

❑ GENUINE—Truthful and authentic
  ◊ How much am I honest, sincere, open, and reliable with the other person?
  ◊ How much is he or she honest, sincere, open, and reliable with me?

❑ RESPECTFUL—Self-determination
  ◊ How much do I honor the other person's right to make his or her own choices and to be responsible for them—even if I disagree with the choices?
  ◊ How much does the other person honor my right to make my own choices and to be responsible for them—even if he or she disagrees with my choices?

❑ EMPATHETIC—Thoughtful understanding
  ◊ How much do I care about the other person—do I really listen and strive to understand his or her emotions, fears, and desires?
  ◊ How much does the other person care about me—does he or she really listen to me and strive to understand my emotions, fears, and desires?

❑ ACCEPTING—Acknowledgment without judgment
  ◊ How much do I fully accept the other person—without criticizing or imposing my expectations and values?
  ◊ How much does the other person fully accept me as I am—without criticizing or imposing his or her expectations and values?

❑ TRUSTFUL—Well-intentioned
  ◊ How much do I believe in the good-hearted intents of the other person—do I appreciate the best about him or her?
  ◊ How much does the other person believe in my good-hearted intents—does he or she appreciate the best about me?

Once you have scored each of the five qualities, calculate the total average score for each person. When we have a GENUINE, RESPECTFUL, EMPATHETIC, ACCEPTING, and TRUSTFUL relationship, the scores usually fall in a range of "8" or above. Really strong and caring friendships average "9" or higher for both individuals.

Incidentally, this is one way to determine how much love there is in a relationship. Although love can be experienced as an emotional interaction between two people, it is also demonstrated in the GREAT relationship qualities. Whether they are conscious of it or not, both individuals in loving relationships continually cultivate all five of these qualities of deep friendship and love. This is also true for every sustained and committed relationship.

By contrast, if friends or partners have difficulties, we can determine which of the GREAT qualities have become problematic. Usually, when one quality suffers, such as a lack of genuineness and honesty, it is likely that the other qualities will also decline. When partners "fall out of love," they have allowed their relationship qualities to erode.

Be aware that even strong relationships have periodic ups and downs. Even the best friendships, family relations, or partnerships will go through challenging times. At times, our scores may be less than an "8." However, all relationships, friendships, and loving partnerships always have the capacity to resolve interpersonal problems and bounce back. We can continue to foster satisfying and enjoyable relationships by consistently striving to be GENUINE, RESPECTFUL, EMPATHETIC, ACCEPTING, and TRUSTFUL.

RESTORING RELATIONSHIPS

Problems arise when one or more of the five GREAT qualities starts to slide—and continues sliding. When this happens, other troubles become apparent. Perhaps we become irritated more often. We might emotionally withdraw from the other person. If the relationship is not restored, the two individuals can drift apart or have a falling out.

However, it usually takes just one of the two individuals to begin restoring the relationship. Often, the most successful approach is to be more empathetic. We do this by striving to better understand the cause of the problems and the other person's feelings. If he or she has felt any combination of the AGRUP feelings—ACCUSED, GUILTY, REJECTED, UNLOVABLE, or POWERLESS (Chapter 6)—then we can explore how to create more WAC feelings (WORTHY, ACCEPTABLE, and CAPABLE; Chapter 8) for both of us.

By doing this, we also gain a better understanding of our own feelings. If we empathetically value each other, our problems and misunderstandings will be resolved. Every disagreement can be healed when we are willing to become more GENUINE, RESPECTFUL, EMPATHETIC, ACCEPTING, and TRUSTFUL (GREAT). And, when we work through our problems, we jointly strengthen our Positive Core Beliefs.

The five GREAT qualities of relationships are skills that we all possess. We can nurture our relationships by consistently practicing these skills. As we strengthen them, we will also more fully appreciate others, and we will increase our ability to develop mutually beneficial, partnering friendships. Whether at work or in our families, with our friends or even our casual relations, our ability to successfully interact with others can constantly improve.

Another aspect of becoming more skilled in the GREAT qualities is the influence these qualities have on our sense of self. Notice that each of the five qualities can be stated as a Positive Core Belief:

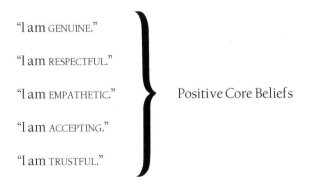

"I am GENUINE."

"I am RESPECTFUL."

"I am EMPATHETIC."   Positive Core Beliefs

"I am ACCEPTING."

"I am TRUSTFUL."

Additionally, each of these five qualities has other associated Positive Core Beliefs:

❑ If we are GENUINE, we can say,
"I am honest, I am sincere, I am reliable, and I am authentic."

❑ If we are RESPECTFUL, we can say,
"I am considerate and I am reasonable."

❑ If we are EMPATHETIC, we can say,
"I am caring, I am listening, and I am understanding."

❑ If we are ACCEPTING, we can say,
"I am affirming, I am supportive, and I am nonjudgmental."

❑ If we are TRUSTFUL, we can say,
"I am encouraging, I am believing, I am trusting, and I am hopeful."

It is important to understand that these skills and the related Positive Core Beliefs should not be associated with being naïve. As we more fully develop these skills, we still have the intelligent capacity to avoid being to be taken advantage of. Actually, the five qualities and their related Positive Core Beliefs typically make us more aware of individuals who are not GENUINE, RESPECTFUL, EMPATHETIC, ACCEPTING, and TRUSTFUL.

GREAT RELATIONSHIPS PROMOTE INTERNAL CONSISTENCY

As we develop these five GREAT skills and strengthen our Positive Core Beliefs, we become more WAC—WORTHY, ACCEPTABLE, and CAPABLE. The GREAT skills reinforce our Self-Belief Identify and further enable us to believe the Key Core Belief, "I am worthy to be loved."

Together, our skills, values, and Positive Core Beliefs are interrelated and mutually supportive. It is difficult to see how an individual could be genuine and at the same time be dishonest. Conversely, when we are genuine, honest, sincere, and authentic, our values become more integrated with our behaviors.

Also, with an added degree of internal consistency between our values and behaviors, we gain added self-confidence in ourselves as well as in our relationships. This also encourages others to have greater trust and assurance in us. For example, if we increase the skill of being more empathetic with a friend, and this is combined with the other four GREAT qualities, then he or she is likely to feel more assured in a relationship with us. This increased mutual-confidence enriches any partnership.

We all know people who live well and enjoy their lives. We say, "They have it all together." It is no coincidence that these people are friendly with almost everyone. Because they are dependably GENUINE, RESPECTFUL, EMPATHETIC, ACCEPTING, and TRUSTFUL, we can't help but feel comfortable around them. Like them, we all have the opportunity to develop our GREAT qualities.

RESOLVING NEGATIVE CORE BELIEFS OF PAST RELATIONSHIPS

After she had met with her counselor a few times, Denise began to better understand how her prior unsuccessful relationships had influenced her Negative Core Beliefs. In high school, Denise had seen herself as a popular and caring individual who was worthy of love. Somehow the rejection of her three boyfriends had become entwined in the intense emotions of abandonment that she had felt when her father died. Rather than risk feeling rejected, abandoned, and worthless, she shut herself off from any potential romantic relationship.

Denise's concerns grew to be Negative Core Beliefs. As she understood how this had occurred, she explored how she could improve the five GREAT qualities. Because she strongly wanted to develop more satisfying relationships, she was able to transform her negative beliefs into Positive Core Beliefs. Within a few months, she made a lot of progress and began to enjoy having a larger number of friends. When one of these friendships turned romantic, she was still concerned but she was willing to take a chance on building an enduring partnership.

Regardless of our circumstances, we can all improve our relationships with others. We can always become an even better friend to our partner, our family members, our fellow workers, and others. Nothing is better than creating GREAT relationships.

RELATIONSHIPS THAT CANNOT BE GREAT

Regrettably, some relationships are almost always out of balance. When one person is consistently GENUINE, RESPECTFUL, EMPATHETIC, ACCEPTING, and TRUSTFUL but the other is not, the relationship does not work. Some individuals cannot be trusted, cannot be respectful of others' decisions, do not want to understand other people, are critically judgmental, or have no interest in the welfare of others. They might be charming but underneath this veneer, these individuals may lack the ability to sustain truly caring relationships.

In these circumstances, one person cannot make up for the lack of GREAT qualities in another. If someone is in a relationship with a person like this—and the other person has no desire to change—the relationship will not be enjoyable, fulfilling, or loving. This is especially true if there is persistent alcohol or drug addiction or continuing mental, emotional, physical, or sexual abuse.

These relationships are toxic. In many of these situations, caring individuals may think they are insufficiently kind or tolerant. They may blame themselves. Toxic relationships can lead caring individuals to develop a distorted sense of self-doubt and very problematic Negative Core Beliefs.

In one situation, a woman had gone out with a very self-centered person. At first, he was charming and witty. After a few dates, however, he began to be less and less accepting of her. He criticized her ideas as foolish and dismissed some of her accomplishments as unimportant. Before long, she started to question her own intelligence. Fortunately, she realized that his charm and his so-called "superior intellect" was just a screen for his own insecurities, and she moved on.

No one is obligated to remain in a damaging relationship. If we are caught in such a situation, we need to consult with someone we trust. Often, talking over problems with a good friend will help us gain a more accurate perception.

Be aware that destructive relationships are highly stressful and take a toll on the five essentials of HEART-integrated health (HEALTH, EMOTIONS, AWARENESS, RELATIONSHIPS, and TRANSCENDENCE, discussed in chapters 1 and 11). Some circumstances will require professional help. Fortunately, all relational problems can be better understood. Once we understand these highly harmful relationships, we can then consider other more potentially positive courses of action.

OVERCOMING ISOLATION THROUGH A CIRCLE OF SUPPORT

We all rely on others for personal support. Likewise, others rely on us. Children need parents or other caring adults for their physical necessities as well as their emotional and mental well-being. As we develop through childhood, adolescence, and adulthood, almost all of us continue to form supportive personal relationships. These friendships are satisfying and validating when others are GENUINE, RESPECTFUL, EMPATHETIC, ACCEPTING, and TRUSTFUL (GREAT). As they care about us—and—as we care about them, we feel worthy to love and to be loved.

Take a moment to imagine a group of caring friends and family members who are there for us. This could be called our "circle of support." As we become more practiced in using the GREAT qualities, we also develop deeper, more meaningful relationships. In this manner, our circle of support can be strengthened and enlarged. We could include trusted friends to share our ups and downs. For many of us, our circle of support can include our faith in transcendence, God, or a higher power. All of us need a circle of support.

The diagram below illustrates a person in the center who is surrounded by eight supportive family members and friends.

CIRCLE OF SUPPORT

A circle of supportive friends and loved ones does not make us dependent on them. A person who depends too much on others often feels needy, disadvantaged, helpless, weak, or inferior. By contrast, when we enjoy being in jointly beneficial relationships, we feel WAC—WORTHY, ACCEPTABLE, and CAPABLE.

Just as significantly, we need to be supportive of others. For every person in our circle of support, we have the opportunity to also be in their circle of support. It adds meaning to our lives when we know others place their trust in our friendship, and it bolsters a number of Positive Core Beliefs. Relying on others and knowing others can rely on us enhances all mutually GREAT friendships. It also results in added appreciation for others and ourselves. The story of Daniel illustrates how this happens.

DANIEL'S STORY

Daniel knew how to appreciate others. He was blessed by almost everyone in his life. Even in his everyday interactions, such as shopping for groceries, he tried to be GENUINE, RESPECTFUL, EMPATHETIC, ACCEPTING, and TRUSTFUL.

Many people who knew him would have been surprised to learn that Daniel previously had been addicted to both alcohol and pornography for several years. Although he kept his job, he was just going through the motions. During that period of his life, he isolated himself from others and felt completely detached. His wife left him and his children wanted nothing to do with him. Without any real friends, he spent evenings, weekends, and holidays alone in his apartment. He felt powerless to overcome his addictions and helpless to change his life.

While he was in this dismal state, a co-worker introduced him to Alcoholics Anonymous and the 12 Steps. In AA meetings he found people who were rising above alcoholism. They were also offering support to others, like Daniel, who wanted to overcome the terrible mental, emotional, and physical consequences of addiction. These recovering individuals became an important part of Daniel's circle of support. For the first time in many years, he was hopeful and decided to put all his efforts into recovery. It was not easy and, along the way, he made several mistakes.

Happily, his network of friends provided support and acceptance. They understood what he was going through and allowed him to learn from his missteps. When he slipped, they trusted that he would create the right path for his recovery. These friends never gave up on him.

He likewise decided to take advantage of a clinic that offered counseling for his pornography obsession as well as the underlying self-beliefs of his addiction behaviors. His mental health professional helped him work through a number of Negative Core Beliefs. Gradually, he learned how to become more genuine and honest, more respectful of others' choices, more empathetic and understanding of others, more willing to accept others without judging them, and more trustful of others' good intentions, even when they made mistakes. As he cultivated the GREAT qualities, he also decided to help those working through their own compulsively harmful behaviors.

Over time, he was able to renew his relationships with his children, and he became a good friend to his ex-wife. He had a circle of support that continuously expanded as he provided sustaining encouragement to others. He lived a happy and meaningful life that blessed a great number of people. When he died several years later, many people told of the ways he had so helpfully made a difference.

Daniel's story exemplifies how people can turn their lives in a new and positive direction by accepting the support of others and then by becoming a supportive friend themselves. It takes conscious effort to develop GREAT relationships, but the rewards are extraordinary.

HAPPIER AND HEALTHIER

We all have the opportunity to increase the GREAT qualities of our relationships. When we actively look for ways to connect with others in meaningful ways, we build bridges of cooperative success. Not all of us are outgoing extroverts, but each of us can create bonds of friendship that will enrich our lives.

As we do this, we will also construct a more vibrant Self-Belief Identity while enhancing our HEART physical wellness and resilience as well as our mental and emotional well-being. Research has shown that those of us who enjoy GREAT relationships also enjoy added Core-Related Health. Our delight in life is multiplied and we experience extra satisfaction in who we are.

REVIEW ACTIVITY
Chapter 10

Which of the five GREAT qualities—GENUINE, RESPECTFUL, EMPATHETIC, ACCEPTING, and TRUSTFUL—do you think would be most worthwhile for you to more fully develop?

What can you specifically do to improve your GREAT relationships?

Identify everyone in your circle of support. How would you enlarge this circle?

How can you be more engaged in supporting and sustaining others? Who do you think might include you in their circle of support?

You can print out each Chapter Review Activity under the Activities tab at KeyCoreBeliefs.org. At the end of most of the Chapter Review Activities, you'll find a link to additional activities that are available without cost.

NOTES: Use this page to record any thoughts about GREAT relationships.

INSPIRED SOLUTIONS

The Vitality of Forgiveness and Transcendence

The real voyage of discovery is not in seeking new places,
but in seeing with new eyes.

Marcel Proust

HOW CAN WE FIND BETTER WAYS TO COPE WITH STRESS?

Science has identified cortisol as one of the main hormones related to anxiety. Like all other hormones, cortisol is vitally important in certain circumstances. For instance, when we perceive a physical threat to ourselves or others we care about, cortisol enables us to react very quickly. It is a major hormone in our ability to engage the "fight or flight" response. Without this hormone, we would react more slowly and with less energy. When it is needed, cortisol is crucial.

Other helpful hormones released during "fight or flight" experiences—adrenalin (epinephrine) and noradrenalin (norepinephrine)—also enable us to act swiftly when we are alarmed. However, because cortisol is perhaps the most prominent hormone that deals with menacing situations, it is known as "the stress hormone."

Cortisol plays a part in post-traumatic stress and other chronically distressful experiences. Unfortunately, in many of these situations, it can be an obstacle to both physical wellness and emotional well-being. When we get angry, a discharge of cortisol, adrenalin, and noradrenalin prepares us to defend ourselves. Likewise, even if we are only anxious or feel on-edge, cortisol and these other hormones are preemptively released just in case the situation gets worse and we need to rapidly react. Not only is cortisol discharged when we are upset, but if we remain somewhat disturbed, the body continues to produce small amounts of this powerful hormone.

THE CORTISOL DRIP

Steady release of cortisol in small amounts can occur in the following conditions:

❑ Chronic stress (e.g., the pressure of a critical boss)

❑ Persistent worry (e.g., anxiousness about a loved one's increasing use of alcohol or drugs)

❑ Doubts about ourselves or unfavorable comparisons with others (e.g., not measuring up to a parent's expectations)

❑ Unresolved resentment (e.g., continued bitterness about being mistreated by a former friend)

In these and many other circumstances, cortisol and other hormones continue to be released at low levels. A prolonged discharge has a negative impact on both the brain and the body. Over time, the sustained production of these stress-related hormones has been linked to gastrointestinal disease, heart disease, cancer, and other medical problems. People who are continuously anxious, nervous, depressed, upset, irritated, or resentful often face health concerns.

The persistent production of cortisol and hormones keeps our body's systems keyed up—ready to fight or escape. However, we were never meant to be in a constant state of conflict or worry. Marco's story illustrates the toll that constant stress can take on our lives.

MARCO'S STORY

If you had known Marco, you would have said he was living a wonderful life. He had been married for 18 years to a delightful partner, Mariella. They were the parents of two girls, both in their teens. Mariella and Marco had secure jobs and although they did not make a lot of money, they had enough to get along pretty well. Marco had only one serious problem—his older brother, Tony.

Tony and Marco had been close when they were growing up. Though they were two years apart, they shared many of the same interests in sports. Marco saw his older, but smaller brother, as a great friend. After they finished high school, married, and started their own families, Marco and his brother continued to enjoy good times together. They particularly liked to attend sports events.

Their camaraderie came to an abrupt end shortly after their parents were unexpectedly killed in a car accident caused by an intoxicated driver. Marco and Tony dearly loved their parents and the loss was crushing. After a brief lawsuit, the estate received a settlement of a little over $125,000. The total value of their parents' assets was close to $95,000 and with the settlement, it amounted to just over $220,000. This was a lot of money for the two brothers, who had been raised in very modest circumstances.

When his parents died, Marco had only been married to Mariella for two years. He was devastated that his parents would never get to know their daughter, who had been born four months after the accident. When Marco learned of the insurance settlement, he took some comfort in knowing there would be enough money for a down payment on a home. So, he and Mariella began looking at houses for sale.

Meanwhile, as the executor of their parents' estate, Tony faced a number of financial problems associated with his business. He "borrowed" money from his parents' bank account and then moved into their home without first consulting Marco. Two years later, when the estate was settled, instead of receiving about half of the estate's $220,000, or $110,000, Marco received a little more than $38,000.

Not surprisingly, Marco and Mariella were angry. Tony never adequately explained what had happened to the rest of the money except to say that it had been "tied up." And because Tony was facing serious financial concerns with his business, he had little time to worry about Marco. After all, his brother had received a tidy sum of money and could now buy a nice home.

While Mariella was busy taking care of their young daughter, Marco stewed about Tony's betrayal. He broke off all connections with his brother. After purchasing a new home, he did not invite Tony over to their house-warming party. In fact, their house became a constant sore spot. Every time Marco drove up to their home, he could only think about how he and Mariella had been cheated. If Tony had not swindled them, they could have had a much better house. A few years later, they sold their home and moved because Marco could no longer stand to live there.

Tony had tried to reach out to his brother, but Marco had completely cut him off and told him he wanted nothing to do with him. When Tony offered $12,000 as a partial restitution, Marco told him he did not want anything from his cheating brother. Now, 16 years later, Marco was still extremely resentful. Then his health started to deteriorate and it soon became a serious concern.

For a number of years, Marco had experienced heartburn. Antacids usually took care of the problem, but gradually he experienced more frequent and serious episodes. He did not like doctors and avoided them at all costs. However, when Mariella caught him coughing up blood, she immediately made an appointment.

After a few tests, a gastrointestinal specialist diagnosed Marco with ulcers and a pre-cancerous digestive tract condition. His doctor gave him a prescription. She also wrote a recommendation for diet and exercise and a referral to meet with a mental health professional who specialized in Health Integration and trauma resolution.

When Marco saw her recommendations, he said he was not interested in changing his diet, did not want to start exercising, and was absolutely not going to see a shrink. Marco's doctor, an experienced physician, knew how to make an impression on her patients. In response to Marco's objections, she seemingly changed the subject by asking him about his two daughters. He told her how proud he was of them. The first was just beginning her senior year in high school and their second daughter was already 13. The doctor then said, "They seem to be amazing young women. I can't help but wonder how much they are going to miss their father if he is not around to see them grow up."

That question transformed Marco's life. Painfully aware of how much he wished his parents had been alive as his own children had grown up, he was not going to let this happen to his daughters—not if he could help it. He started to exercise and to eat more healthy foods. He also made an appointment to see a mental health professional.

As he met with his counselor, Sharlene, she listened to his life's story and had him fill out a brief questionnaire about any previous unfavorable experiences. She also took the time to explain how gastrointestinal medical issues are often correlated with chronic distress, unresolved trauma, resentment, and other unsettled mental health concerns. She gave him literature to read, helped him devise a plan to reduce his stress at work, and encouraged him to set aside 20 minutes each evening to go for a walk with Mariella. This he was happy to do.

At their next meeting, she reviewed the questionnaire Marco had completed and noticed his bitterness towards his brother. Sharlene asked if he would be willing to work on his resentment. In his mind, Marco wanted to say, "Are you kidding me?" But instead, he heard himself ask, "Does my bitterness have something to do with my health problems?" Intuitively, Marco already knew the answer to his question.

Through diligent effort, Marco worked with Sharlene to remedy his resentment. He applied the principles of HEART Health Integration (Chapter 2). He started to consistently eat better, he took daily walks, and learned how to do brief meditation. His efforts began to ease some of his distress. Mariella was encouraging and supportive. About two months later, he had also resolved the resentment towards his brother, though he was still not in contact with Tony. He began to see real constructive differences in his life.

His youngest daughter was the first to comment on this when she said, "Dad, I don't believe it. You are becoming a new person!" It was not long before he began to feel better than he ever had in his adult life. Negative Core Beliefs, such as, "I am vindictive" that he had clung to, began to be transformed to Positive Core Beliefs. Before the year was out, he achieved a much higher level of comprehensive health. He also decided that it was time to call his brother, Tony. He asked him to go to a football game. After the game, they had a long talk and many old wounds were healed. Not only did he get his brother back, Marco turned off the "cortisol drip."

Chronic distress has an unfavorable impact on our overall Health Integration. The continuous production of low levels of cortisol and other hormones significantly contributes to reduced mental well-being and physical wellness. Whether it is unresolved post-traumatic stress, frustration, resentment, anxiousness, or some other distress—these hormones can adversely alter how well we live and how long we live.

THE COMPARISON PROBLEM

Another problem that plagues many of us occurs when we compare ourselves with others. All of us have engaged in this. Though in some circumstances, evaluating ourselves with others might be helpful, most of the time it just feeds Negative Core Beliefs and weakens our Self-Belief Identity.

Many of us measure our self-esteem by these made-up comparisons. For example:

"He is not very bright."

"She has it all."

"I wish I had a car like that."

"They don't have much money."

"It's too bad their children didn't get more education."

"I wish I were that smart."

"What's wrong with him?"

"Women can't do math."

"Men are so dense."

"Those people are weird."

When we measure ourselves this way, we climb on the "ladder of comparison." We believe we are either above another person ("I'm glad I make more money than he does") or beneath someone else ("I'm just not as smart as she is").

Comparing ourselves with others is the basis of inappropriate pride. This leads us to become biased and to prejudge others. When we do this, and we all do at some time, we climb on the ladder of comparison. Whether we compare ourselves positively or negatively, this becomes a measure of our "vertical self-esteem." Our self-esteem is then determined by how far up we are—and how many people are either beneath us or above us. By the way, this has nothing to do with our true self-worth.

When individuals are "up the ladder," they need to climb ever higher in order to validate their self-esteem. But no matter how high they get, they still know that others are above them. No one is ever content with this self-esteem because it always depends on the ability to climb above others. Climbing up the ladder creates a continuous degree of anxiety because of the constant risk that we will not be able to keep up with others who are also striving to climb to the top. This anxiousness also slowly releases cortisol and other stress-related hormones.

When people are "down the ladder," they look up at others who appear to have greater advantages than they do. This may motivate some individuals to do better. However, it more frequently becomes a source of resentment and frustration. Some people believe that they are deprived in comparison to those who have more education, money, power, self-esteem, accomplishments, etc. It creates a never-ending cycle of feeling less than others and feeds the Negative Core Belief, "I am not enough." This kind of distress also produces the slow drip of cortisol.

THE DEVELOPMENT OF SELF-WORTH

As discussed in Chapter 8, the concept of true self-worth acknowledges that everyone deserves to have human dignity. Instead of climbing a ladder, we choose to honor the value of others and, at the same time, honor our own value. How much money others make, the clothes they wear, where they live, or what other people think about them is of little concern to us because we have a comfortable

Self-Belief Identity. We don't need to compare ourselves with others because we are satisfied with who we are.

Since we all have innate worth regardless of what we do, how much we earn, or how successful we become, no one needs a ladder of comparison. As one individual said, "When I get impatient with a driver who is driving too slowly, I know I am up on the ladder of comparison. As I become aware of this, I have the option to stay on the ladder or to get off. When I recognize the worth of the other driver, my blood pressure goes down and I move on to enjoy the rest of my day."

We all possess a unique combination of characteristics, qualities, and experiences. However, we have no reason ever to see ourselves as either better or worse than someone else. Indeed, as we shed the need to compare ourselves with others, we become more interested in learning from other individuals and sharing positive experiences with them. When we know we have inherent self-worth, we continue to grow and continue to develop added Positive Core Beliefs.

As we consider our lives, it is worth asking:

- ❏ Are we too concerned with what others think of us?
- ❏ Are we afraid of being judged by others?
- ❏ Do we strive never to make mistakes because we would look foolish?
- ❏ Do we want others to see only our strengths and never our weaknesses?
- ❏ Do we need the approval of others to feel good about ourselves?
- ❏ How important is our appearance?

    Or:

- ❏ Are we comfortable being who we are?
- ❏ Do we refuse to pass judgment on others?
- ❏ Do we believe it is okay for everyone to make and learn from mistakes?
- ❏ Do we continually work towards improving the quality of our relationships?
- ❏ Do we recognize those times when we make comparisons with others?
- ❏ Do we make consistent effort to appreciate the worth of others and ourselves?

Comparing ourselves to others is pointless. As one person noted, "What I think about you is none of your business. It's my business. And, what you think about me is none of my business. It's yours." Our true self-worth is based on seeing ourselves as caring individuals. Wouldn't it be better if we valued everyone as a person of worth? It is up to us to make that choice every day.

In Marco's story, it is easy to understand how he compared himself to his sibling. On many occasions, he said to himself, "At least I am not like my cheating brother." As he worked with his counselor, Marco discovered that he compared himself with many others. For example, he was rarely satisfied with the work of those he supervised and often looked down on them. He also took great pride in the fact that he was two positions higher in his company than a person who was employed at the same time he was hired.

On the other hand, he was lower on the ladder in many situations. Marco thought his house was not big enough, his daughter was not as talented as his neighbor's, his wife got a bigger bonus than he did, and his old high school friend drove a more expensive car. Marco was forever getting on the comparison ladder. Much of the time he was down the ladder looking up at others who were doing better.

Once he began to realize just how much of his life was focused on these comparisons, he learned how to reorient his thinking by using empathy. He took the time to understand his subordinates better. As he connected with them, they became more productive and his work team's performance began to noticeably improve. When his daughter brought home a report card with three B's and two C's, he took the time to sit down and listen to her problems at school. He also quit worrying about what others thought of his home, his income, the clothes he wore, or the car he drove.

He was freed from the comparisons that had previously weighed him down. As this became his new reality, Marco replaced old, negative beliefs with Positive Core Beliefs and he became more comfortable with his true self-worth. Not coincidentally, his ulcers healed and his health greatly improved.

THE RESENTMENT REMEDY

Resentment is commonly used to describe grudges, the need for revenge, the settling of scores, payback, or vengeance. In any of its forms, resentment produces cortisol and other hormones that have long-term, negative side effects on our bodies and reduce our resilience to disease.

Of course, resentment has a purpose. It is a defense mechanism to keep us on guard. No one wants to be taken advantage of—particularly not a second time. In other words, resentment acts as a radar to ensure that we will not be fooled again. It also creates a wide variety of unhelpful behaviors. Examples include the cold shoulder one partner gives the other for forgetting a birthday, the craving for revenge because we have been fired, and the need to get even with a person who humiliated us. Our desire for justice and retribution can become all-consuming.

Indeed, when we look at criminal behavior or at the history of warfare, quite frequently we see revenge and resentment playing out in the lives of individuals, families, communities, and nations. The examples are numerous and the tremendous costs in human suffering impossible to count.

However, Marco was aware of how much damage his resentment had caused. He learned how his past bitterness towards his brother had played havoc with his digestive system. He also understood the other costs that were borne by his wife, his daughters, and others. His sour moods, disapproving reactions, and flashes of anger impacted everyone around him.

Marco's counselor introduced the one sure remedy for resentment—forgiveness. At first, Marco did not want to hear anything about forgiving his brother. There was no way he was going to let Tony off the hook for what he had done. However, his counselor helped him see that forgiving Tony was primarily for Marco's benefit.

USING FORGIVENESS TO FREE OURSELVES FROM THE OFFENSES OF OTHERS

When harm is done to us, we want justice for the hurt that we have suffered. This is a natural reaction for just about all of us, and it was true for Collin. His teenage daughter was killed in a drunk-driving accident. The driver of the car, also a teen, was arrested for DUI, tried and found guilty, and sentenced to prison. For months, Collin was extremely bitter. He thought the young man should have received a harsher sentence. He wanted this individual to suffer as much as he had suffered from the death of his daughter.

After some time, Collin realized how much of his life centered on his bitterness and resentment towards this teenager. His thoughts and feelings were predominantly dark and hateful. He became aware that he spent much more time thinking about vengeance than he did about the loving relationship he had previously had with his daughter.

As a person of faith, he asked God to help him resolve the hate in his heart. It was not immediate, but over time he began to feel greater love for his daughter and less rancor towards the offender. At a later date, he arranged to meet the man in prison. He stated simply and sincerely, "I want you to know that I forgive you." After this encounter, he noted how liberating this had been for him. Only then could he move on with his life. His Negative Core Belief, "I am vengeful," was transformed into one of the most Positive Core Beliefs: "I am forgiving."

THE SNARE OF REVENGE

Unfortunately, some of us live a great deal of our lives ensnared by feelings of retaliation, revenge, or payback. Giving in to these feelings can be devastating and can leave us feeling cynical and embittered. Many of us stay trapped in resentment because we refuse to forgive. Nevertheless, our hurts can be healed, and we can live a fulfilling life. The need for vindictiveness, justice, revenge, or a day of reckoning can be replaced with healing. When we let go of the demand for vengeance or payback, we are on the right track to forgive.

Forgiving can be simply defined:

Forgiveness occurs when we willingly give up our need

for others to suffer for what they have done.

As we consider this, we may realize that we have on occasion offended others. When we become more forgiving, we also become more open to receiving forgiveness for ourselves. If we resolve bitter feelings towards others, we become more compassionate and caring. In addition, our Positive Core Beliefs increase and we more fully accept that we are worthy to be loved.

Misconceptions about forgiveness

Five mistaken notions about forgiving are critically important to understand:

❑ FORGIVING IS NOT ABOUT FORGETTING. The old saying "forgive and forget" is nearly impossible to implement because we have no direct control over our memories. Also, in order to learn from previous harmful experiences, we need to remember them in order to avoid getting caught up in similar circumstances. However, relentlessly harsh memories can be changed through forgiving. One of the indications of forgiveness occurs when our memories are no longer bitter.

❑ FORGIVING IS NOT ABOUT EXCUSING. Bad behavior is bad behavior. Offenses should not be ignored, swept under the rug, or rationalized away. For example, criminal behavior can be forgiven by the person who was victimized but this does not mean the offender is exempt from justice. Just as importantly, when someone takes advantage of us or our loved ones, we can forgive without excusing or condoning their offending behaviors. Sometimes we refuse to forgive because we think that equates it with pardoning the wrongdoer.

❑ FORGIVING IS NOT ABOUT TRUSTING. Trust is totally independent from forgiveness. It must be earned over time. Clearly, it would be a mistake to trust someone who was likely to repeat offensive or dishonest behaviors. We can forgive others, but our forgiveness is completely separate from trusting them.

❑ FORGIVING IS NOT ABOUT RENEWING A HARMFUL RELATIONSHIP. If it is likely that an offending person will continue to act harmfully, we have no obligation to mend this injurious association. Unfortunately, ending a relationship may be necessary even if the person is a friend, a loved one, or a member of our family. If someone is unsafe for us or our loved ones, we should not associate with him or her. Nevertheless, we can forgive someone without being in a relationship with that person.

❑ FORGIVING IS NOT ABOUT WAITING FOR AN APOLOGY FROM THE OTHER PERSON. We have no control over whether someone is remorseful or if that person will ever apologize. However, some of us refuse to forgive others until they offer an apology. In this situation, we might have to wait forever because some offenders will never say, "I am sorry." By making our forgiveness conditional in this way, we let others have power over us and we carry the burden of our resentment indefinitely. On the contrary, we can forgive even if another never apologizes.

When we harbor feelings of hostility, vengeance, or anger towards another, we let the offending person keep us stuck in our own destructive feelings. These bitter feelings may preoccupy us with dreams of justice or revenge, which can become an obsessive pattern of never-ending, negative emotions. In the meantime, the toxic cortisol continues to drip.

When we refuse to forgive, we drink a venom of our own making. If we hold on to our grudges, we cannot feel wholehearted and we reduce mental and physical health. Resentment is an emotional state that causes the body to be on guard. Those who hold resentments are more prone to diseases and disorders.

By contrast, individuals who consistently practice forgiveness live healthier, happier, and more meaningful lives. The primary purpose of forgiving is to make ourselves whole. Forgiveness always benefits the forgiver. After truly forgiving someone who has harmed us, we no longer need to mentally carry that person around with us. In some situations, our forgiveness may restore a relationship and the other person may feel forgiven. But even if this does not happen, and often this is the case, we will still be liberated from our bitterness.

As we forgive others, we resolve our resentment and then it is possible to move on with our life.

THE PROCESS OF FORGIVING OTHERS

There is no one right way to forgive, but the steps outlined below have worked for many.

1. Remember an event when someone offended or hurt you. Hold that memory as just a single snapshot in your mind.

2. At that time, did you feel any of the AGRUP feelings—ACCUSED, GUILTY, REJECTED, UNLOVABLE, or POWERLESS? Specifically identify each of your underlying feelings and recognize the resulting secondary emotions of anger, sadness, or fear.

3. Remember, you are a loving, caring person.

4. Ask, "Did this person intend to be hurtful?" If the answer is "no," then now is the time to let go of this. If you believe this person did intend to be hurtful, decide if you now want to let go of this negative influence in your life.

5. Examine, "Do I need to hold on to my resentment because it serves some purpose for me?" Also ask, "Would I be better off if I could let go of my need for the other person to suffer for my sake?"

6. Ask, "What can I do to help me forgive?" This might include meditation, mindfulness, prayer, etc. Try to visualize the positive impact of forgiving this person. How would this constructively impact you?

7. Use empathy to understand the other person's hurt. Did he or she feel ACCUSED, GUILTY, REJECTED, UNLOVABLE, or POWERLESS before the offense? The vast majority of individuals do not knowingly offend others unless they experience one or more of these feelings. Empathy helps us understand the other person, and this is often crucial to forgiving. However, to empathize with the other person's feelings does not mean we excuse their behavior. We are simply trying to better understand them.

8. If you no longer need the other individual to suffer for what he or she did, then you can explore what would be in your best interests and also the best interests of the other person. For example, it might include offering a prayer for that person and yourself or creating a positive thought for both of you.

9. If you played a part in creating the offense, take responsibility for only what you did and resolve not to repeat this. Apologize and make amends if this is the right thing to do. While not easy, many people report this step was essential to their own healing even if the other individual did not reciprocate.

10. Remember to be patient with yourself. Forgiving often takes time but making an effort to forgive is positive. If you continue to practice forgiveness, you will find a greater measure of peace, understanding, and resolution.

Countless individuals have testified to the positive power of forgiveness. Forgiving others is one of the most valuable ways to improve our lives.

RECEIVING FORGIVENESS—WHY WE SHOULD STOP PUNISHING OURSELVES

Also, when we forgive others, we are more open to receive forgiveness for ourselves. As we consistently exercise forgiveness, we feel more WAC—WORTHY, ACCEPTABLE, and CAPABLE. We quit trying to earn our own forgiveness through self-punishment. What a relief that is!

Trying to punish ourselves for something we did wrong really does not work. No matter how much we self-punish, it never seems to be enough and only reinforces our Negative Core Beliefs. On the other hand, when we forgive others and give up our need for them to suffer, we can also free ourselves from punishing ourselves. This also aligns our values and our behaviors. It helps us learn from our mistakes, offer appropriate amends, and work towards not repeating the same errors.

In forgiving and receiving forgiveness, we unshackle ourselves from previous · harms and hurts. Only then can we be truly free of the past so that we can live in the present.

How to open yourself to receiving forgiveness

We can all benefit from receiving forgiveness and letting go of self-punishment. This is very similar to the process of forgiving others. It does not depend on whether the individuals we offended have forgiven us. They may not be able to forgive. However, we can still benefit from self-forgiveness if we follow an approach such as this one:

1. Remember a time when you hurt or offended someone. Hold that memory as just a single snapshot in your mind.

2. At that time, did you feel any of the AGRUP feelings—ACCUSED, GUILTY, REJECTED, UNLOVABLE, or POWERLESS? Specifically identify each of your underlying feelings and recognize the resulting secondary emotions of anger, sadness, or fear. This allows you to see the circumstances more clearly, but it does not excuse or justify your misbehavior.

3. Remember, you are a loving, caring person.

4. Ask, "Did I intend to be hurtful?" If the answer is "no," then now is the time to let go of the need for you to suffer or punish yourself. If you believe you intended to be hurtful, do you now want to remove this negative influence from your life?

5. Examine, "Do I need to hold on to the need to punish myself because it serves some purpose for me?" Also ask, "Would I be better off if I could let go of my need for self-punishment at this time?"

6. Ask, "What can I do that would help me receive forgiveness?" This might include meditation, mindfulness, prayer, etc. Try to visualize the positive impact of being forgiven. How would this constructively help you?

7. If it is appropriate, make amends by asking for forgiveness and make suitable restitution. However, be mindful that in some situations it may not yet be the right time to ask for forgiveness or to attempt restitution because the other person is still upset and unforgiving. However, you can always work to be GREAT—more GENUINE, RESPECTFUL, EMPATHETIC, ACCEPTING, and TRUSTFUL of the good-hearted nature of others. Becoming a better person increases the likelihood of finding the right moment to ask for forgiveness.

8. If you no longer want to punish yourself, then you can explore what would be in your best interests and in the best interests of the other person. For example, it might include doing something positive for the person you offended. However, you should not intrude on someone who is not ready to forgive you.

9. Because you played a part in this offense, be responsible for what you did and resolve not to repeat this. However, do not take responsibility for the actions of any other person.

10. Remember to be patient. Just attempting to receive forgiveness is positive. You may not immediately feel forgiven but in time you will find a greater sense of peace.

We know we have forgiven or received forgiveness when we no longer feel the need for someone else to suffer or the need for self-punishment. The bitterness of past offences is resolved and our heart is transformed. When we continually practice the skill of forgiving, we develop a spirit of compassion for others and ourselves.

Not everyone wants to forgive—it is a choice. Each one of us must determine if the benefits of forgiving outweigh the consequences of wanting others or ourselves to continue suffering.

TRANSCENDENCE

In Chapter 2, we discussed Health Integration and the five essentials of HEART.

❑   HEALTH—physical wellness based on the principles of healthy living
❑   EMOTIONS—emotional balance and enjoyment through self-understanding
❑   AWARENESS—conscious use of our mental abilities
❑   RELATIONSHIPS—caring and satisfying connections with others
❑   TRANSCENDENCE—enrichment through inspiring and uplifting influences

The fifth HEART essential, TRANSCENDENCE, relies on engaging in reassuring, encouraging, heartening, or inspiring experiences. We often become transcendent by our sense of appreciation, wonder, and enjoyment. Through transcendence, we go beyond self-imposed limitations to enjoy higher attributes of love, caring, and understanding.

Transcendence could occur when we are moved by a beautiful sunset, uplifting music, a work of art, prayerful meditation, or a walk in a forest. Many find transcendence in religious participation. For some of us, it is the revitalizing sense of being surrounded by nature. For others, it might be the regular practice of yoga, meditative mindfulness, deep breathing, prayer, or spiritual study. It often includes the indescribable feeling of being close to a friend, listening to the laughter of a child, singing with loved ones, or the companionship of a pet. When we feel moved with love and gratitude, we feel a sense of transcendence and we value who we are.

Even for those who have dismissed transcendence as unimportant, it can still become a vibrant aspect of living life well. Studies demonstrate that those who sense awe-inspiring experiences feel more whole within themselves and more connected to others and to the world around them. Finding transcendence can play an energizing and inspiring role in our lives.

All three of the authors of this book are engaged in religious faiths and we appreciate our associations with those in our faith-based communities. However, even more meaningful for us is the uplifting inspiration we enjoy that goes beyond our religious affiliations. We find transcendence in many facets of our lives.

CREATING AN UPLIFTING LIFE

Everyone can benefit from transcendent experiences. We know someone who feels a strong sense of being one with nature when she hikes. She attends church and meditates. She loves inspiring books and sets aside time to read each day. Her pet is a joy to her. Every morning she goes outside for a few minutes to enjoy the weather regardless if it is hot or cold, clear or stormy. She rejoices in the love she shares with others. Daily, she gives inner thanks for the blessings and challenges of her life. In all of these transcendent experiences, she finds hope and harmony.

Another person regularly leaves his busy workday schedule for half an hour to listen to music. He does not play a musical instrument and his singing voice is off-key, but this does not stop him from enjoying rock and roll, classical symphonies, jazz, and mariachi bands. Regardless of what he listens to, he always finds himself leaving his daily demands behind while being transported by the music he loves. This is just one way he creates transcendence in his life.

We can increase our openness to uplifting experiences by focusing on enriching interactions. Take a few minutes to consider the following questions:

❑ **A**PPRECIATE: Constantly look for opportunities to be grateful.
  ◊ What brings you an added measure of thankfulness?
  ◊ How can you express gratitude for the simple pleasures of your life?
  ◊ What can you do to better appreciate your friends and loved ones?

❑ **W**ONDER: Make a choice to view the world through eyes of wonder.
  ◊ What brings out a greater sense of curiosity or admiration in you?
  ◊ In what ways can you increase your sense of wonder by discovering the amazing beauty of art, the harmony of music, or the smile of a stranger?
  ◊ How can you become more aware of the colors of a single flower, the ever-changing cloud formations, or the warmth of the sun?

❑ **E**NJOY: Become a master at creating delight.
  ◊ What brings you delighted satisfaction?
  ◊ How can you produce added enjoyment for yourself?
  ◊ What can you do to increase enjoyment for others?
  ◊ What would enable you to discover greater gladness?

Each of us shapes the world in which we live. Sometimes it takes focused effort to rise above the difficulties we encounter. Though sometimes challenging, regardless of our circumstances, we can increase our AWE—APPRECIATION, WONDER, and ENJOYMENT.

THE VITALITY OF EMBRACING FORGIVENESS AND TRANSCENDENCE

Earlier in this chapter, we presented Marco's story. Recall that his mental health counselor encouraged him to engage in meditation as a part of his path to greater emotional and physical health. Marco found meditation to be an important way to relax after coming home from work and much more effective than turning on the TV. His daily walks also proved to be valuable in reducing stress and increasing his energy.

In addition, he created comforting peace by forgiving Tony. Marco's newfound degree of greater harmony developed into a profoundly different life perspective. At first, he had a hard time grasping how these changes had made a difference for him. However, he soon began to understand that forgiveness and transcendence had given him a more wholehearted outlook on his life. He discovered more personal fulfillment and enjoyment than he had ever known.

Similarly, he discovered that his life had an added vitality. He literally felt more alive. It was an amazing aspect of learning how to forgive and how to become transcendent. When he recognized how this had changed his life, he determined that he was never going back to his past practices because his life now was so much more satisfying. Marco determined to cultivate what his counselor called "the spirit of forgiveness" and "the practice of transcendence."

The spirit of forgiveness is a commitment to forgive others and receive forgiveness for ourselves as soon as it is feasible to do so. The practice of transcendence is the daily application of one or more uplifting activities.

MARCO'S OTHER STORY

Marco learned that developing the spirit of forgiveness and transcendence could be quite a challenge. This happened one day when a colleague at work criticized him in front of others. He was enraged. Not only was she wrong, but she had no right to disparage him when others were present.

That night, Marco remembered the forgiveness steps he had used to deal with past events such as Tony's dishonesty. At first, he wanted to hold on to his "justifiable anger," but he had already committed to use the spirit of forgiveness. It took almost an hour to calm himself with meditation and then to work through the forgiveness steps. As he did this, he was surprised to realize that he had done something to trigger her criticism.

After recognizing how he had contributed to the problem, he felt prompted to write a simple letter of apology to his colleague. The next day, as he walked into work, he ran into her. Fortunately, he was prepared. As he handed her the note of apology he said, "Until I had a chance to think about what happened yesterday, I didn't understand how I had played a part in the problem. I apologize. When you feel good about talking over the situation, maybe we could chat for a few minutes so that I could get a better grasp of your side of the situation." His colleague replied, "Let me think about it." Later that day, they resolved the problem.

Some people might think that Marco was weak in apologizing. After all, his colleague should not have criticized him in front of others. But Marco had determined to always work through issues sooner rather than later. He knew that in the past he would have harbored great resentment for his colleague and this would have only created more problems. Marco had enough experience with Tony and others to understand that resentment was totally ineffective.

Employing forgiveness and transcendence, he not only resolved the concern, he also found how to create better work results that increased efficiency. In doing this, he reinforced his Positive Core Beliefs—"I am WORTHY to be loved," "I am ACCEPTABLE," and "I am CAPABLE."

Every one of us has the ability to cultivate the spirit of forgiveness and the practice of transcendence. As we incorporate a transcendent way of living, the other four HEART essentials are positively influenced. We gain a greater measure of HEALTH, we more effectively regulate the stress hormones of our EMOTIONS, we increase our ability to use the mental reasoning abilities of our AWARENESS, and we measurably improve the quality of our RELATIONSHIPS. This compound effect also amplifies the strength of our Positive Core Beliefs and Self-Belief Identity, and our overall Core-Related Health is bolstered.

It is crucial to consider just how vital our lives can be as we more fully integrate HEART wellness and well-being with Positive Core Beliefs. As mental health professionals, the three of us have witnessed how transcendence has constructively influenced thousands of individuals. It has also been amazing to witness these influences in each of our own lives.

REVIEW ACTIVITY
Chapter 11

Some questions to consider:

Has anyone offended you whom you need to forgive?

How would you benefit by practicing forgiveness?

In the past, have you been able to let go of the need to punish yourself?

When have you felt a greater sense of appreciation, wonder, or enjoyment in your life?

What transcendence practices have you regularly engaged in that provided uplifting influences?

What additional transcendent practices would be worth considering?

You can print out each Chapter Review Activity under the Activities tab at KeyCoreBeliefs.org. At the end of most of the Chapter Review Activities, you'll find a link to additional activities that are available without cost.

NOTES: Use this page to record any thoughts you have about forgiveness and transcendence.

CHAPTER 12

CORE-RELATED HEALTH

A Heartfelt Perspective

*There will come a time when you believe
everything is finished. That will be the beginning.*

Louis L'Amour

HOW DO THE HEART ESSENTIALS AND POSITIVE CORE BELIEFS BUILD HAPPINESS?

Core-Related Health encourages us to create a comprehensive approach to living. This requires our Self-Belief Identity to be based on Positive Core Beliefs and it includes the five HEART essentials of Health Integration (HEALTH, EMOTIONS, AWARENESS, RELATIONSHIPS, and TRANSCENDENCE).

THE FUNDAMENTALS OF CORE-RELATED HEALTH

❑ A Self-Belief Identity based on predominantly Positive Core Beliefs

❑ Health Integration that includes the five HEART essentials (HEALTH, EMOTIONS, AWARENESS, RELATIONSHIPS, and TRANSCENDENCE)

Complete physical wellness and emotional well-being only occur when these fundamentals are combined.

At the beginning of this book, we discussed how our sense of who we are—our Self-Belief Identity—relies on the beliefs we have about ourselves. Our Key Core Beliefs are crucial to our perceptions, emotions, thinking, and behaving. As we develop Positive Core Beliefs and replace any Negative Core Beliefs, we also strengthen a constructive Self-Belief Identity.

In addition, we reviewed the five interrelated essentials of physical wellness and emotional well-being—Health Integration through the five HEART essentials, listed in the box on the next page.

THE ESSENTIALS OF HEALTH INTEGRATION

Health—physical wellness based on the principles of healthy living

Emotions—emotional balance through self-understanding

Awareness—conscious use of our mental abilities

Relationships—caring and satisfying connections with others

Transcendence—enrichment through inspiring and uplifting influences

As we discussed in Chapter 2, the HEART essentials greatly contribute to the development of Positive Core Beliefs. The central importance of these interconnected essentials has been understood for many years. In the United States, a number of medical practices were established in the 1960s to promote all of the characteristics of healthful living. Integrated health initiatives all over the globe have recognized how these vital elements help us all live better, longer, healthier, and more meaningful lives. When combined with a strong Self-Belief Identity based on Positive Core Beliefs, we establish true Core-Related Health.

One area of research that author and explorer Dan Buettner highlights in his books describes "Blue Zones." These Blue Zones are locations around the world where a higher percentage of people live to be a hundred years or more. Rather than residing in assisted living or nursing homes, these people live independently. They are vigorously healthy and active in their communities. Unsurprisingly, they take good care of their bodies (HEALTH), enjoy heartfelt EMOTIONS, are continually cognitively aware and engaged (AWARENESS), relish close RELATIONSHIPS with friends and family, and practice mindfulness, religious observance, or meditation (TRANSCENDENCE)—they are HEART healthy!

This degree of integrated wellness and well-being is available to each of us, regardless of our age or circumstances. And while we live in complex times filled with responsibilities and pressures, nevertheless, we have the opportunity to create increased joy and meaning through Core-Related Health.

Jim, one of the coauthors of this book, relates how these factors greatly influenced his wellness and well-being.

JIM'S EXPERIENCE

Many years ago, a person told me that he attended a group called Adult Children of Alcoholics. He explained this was a group of adults who were raised in a family with an alcoholic parent. I told him that was interesting but I thought this did not apply to me. I was 40 at the time and never saw myself as coming from a family with "issues."

Fortunately, I later attended a program on Adult Children of Alcoholics presented by Sharon Wegscheider-Cruse, founding chair of the National Association for Children of Alcoholics. She showed a video entitled "Another Chance," about a woman in a therapy program dealing with emotional issues concerning her family when she was a child. She remembered repressed feelings that had been locked inside of herself for many years.

Suddenly, I recognized that I had many of these same repressed emotions. For the first time in my life, I understood the hurt and pain that I had suppressed. I realized that my father was not only an alcoholic and a compulsive gambler, he was also a sex addict. My mother was a very depressed woman. In addition, she physically abused me until I was 13.

After watching that video, I recognized that I had a number of Negative Core Beliefs that caused me a great deal of distress. For example, I had a major need for approval from my parents but they never gave it to me. Regardless of my achievements in education, my professional accomplishments, and the success of my marriage, they did not express any support. I never realized that I had worked so hard to get their approval. For many years, I was compulsive in my drive to "do good."

Once I understood that I was working overtime for my parents' expression of support, I stepped back. Instead of obsessively driving myself to take care of others, I began to focus more on self-healing. As I was doing this, I was also able to share this healing with my clients, my wife, and our children.

Despite my efforts, however, my Negative Core Beliefs were still locked inside my body in what I refer to as "trigger points." Around 1990, my body began to stiffen up, and by 1994 the muscles in my right arm and hips became frozen with symptoms similar to cerebral palsy. Apparently, a car accident many years before had created a Mild Traumatic Brain Injury, but the doctors did not have the ability at that time to diagnose this.

It looked like I would be in a wheelchair the rest of my life. However, in 1995, I consulted with a massage therapist about Neuromuscular Therapy. This therapeutic approach frees people from overactive physical trigger points that immobilize them. Over a three-month period, she systematically released the trigger points in my body. Each time this occurred, I would have flashbacks of childhood events. These flashbacks represented the captured distressful experiences of my life in these bodily trigger points. After a few months, I regained full mobility of my arm, hips, and legs.

Despite a few relapses, I have become more emotionally and mentally resilient. Today, I am healthier because of the development of my resulting Positive Core Beliefs. However, when I deal with high levels of distress, such as a serious illness that my wife had, I sometimes have to contend with physical weaknesses. I am convinced that we need to do all that we can to strengthen our Positive Core Beliefs and take care of every aspect of our Core-Related Health.

When we actively choose to foster the HEART essentials, we continue to strengthen our Positive Core Beliefs. The more we become conscious of any Negative Core Beliefs and transform them, the more we develop a resilient Self-Belief Identity. We live with less fear and enjoy a higher level of empathy, connection, and caring. Altogether, this enriches our Core-Related Health.

Studies have repeatedly shown the value of combining the practice of medicine with counseling. Total health outcomes significantly improve through the combined treatment of doctors, other healthcare specialists, and mental health professionals. Working as a team and partnering with their patients, major advances in physical wellness and emotional well-being are becoming more widespread.

For example, more and more physicians are employing mental health professionals to augment the effectiveness of their medical practices. As we better appreciate the amazing interconnectivity of the mind, the brain, and the body, we can all benefit from professional services that offer Core-Related Health wellness and well-being.

AN EXAMPLE OF CORE-RELATED HEALTH

A woman in her 40s had suffered from an undiagnosed neurological condition since she was a child. Certain noises were unbearably loud—if someone were munching on popcorn or eating a sandwich, the sound was so loud that she couldn't tolerate it. As a child, even moderate sounds were so intense that her frustrations frequently turned into exasperated fury. It was obvious to her that others were not bothered by these noises so she desperately tried to hide this excruciating problem. Throughout her life, she constantly felt isolated, anxious, and helpless. She was dreadfully ashamed and terrified that others would learn her closely guarded secret. Despite being surrounded by loving friends and family members, she felt terribly alone.

Fortuitously, she learned of someone with a similar condition. After a medical evaluation, she was diagnosed with a very rare neurological condition known as misophonia. Misophonia occurs when normal sounds are extremely amplified in the brain. For example, if someone were eating a taco, it might sound like a thunderous rock slide. Unhappily, no known cure exists for this condition.

When she began to understand the cause of so much of the shame in her life, she sought out a mental health professional. Because of her condition, she had developed a number of Negative Core Beliefs. She really thought that she was impaired, broken, and unlovable. Probably her most prevalent Negative Core Beliefs was, "I am crazy." Her mental health professional helped her to develop a number of Positive Core Beliefs including, "Regardless of my condition, I am okay and I am resilient," "I am nurtured by my family and friends," "I am safe," and "I am worthy to be loved."

Before her diagnosis, she could not even confide in her closest friends about it. After revealing her condition to family members and friends, she discovered how much they cared about her. She had a wonderful circle of support. This became her springboard for improved relationships and growing happiness. Already successful in many aspects of her life, every day became a new adventure for her.

The opportunity of a lifetime

As noted previously, we can all learn how to live our lives more fully through HEART Health Integration and a Self-Belief Identity based on Positive Core Beliefs. Each of us can gain greater confidence in our most crucial Key Core Belief, "I am worthy to be loved." As we focus on nurturing our GREAT relationships (ones that are GENUINE, RESPECTFUL, EMPATHETIC, ACCEPTING, and TRUSTFUL), we create added enjoyment and fulfillment.

Each of us can develop our own approach to create greater wellness and well-being. As we become more aware of the HEART essentials, we will be more attuned to our needs. We can determine when one or more of the essentials is not working well and we can make course corrections.

We can also develop a circle of support that includes a primary care doctor and perhaps a mental health professional, as well as close family members and friends, a minister, a mentor, or other trusted individuals. It is crucial that we don't face life's stressful challenges by ourselves. All of us can develop a network of individuals who support us and whom we can support.

In doing this, we will add to our emotional well-being through enriching our most important Key Core Beliefs. If we encounter Negative Core Beliefs, we always have the capability to transform them into favorable Positive Core Beliefs

Increasing HEART Health Integration and Positive Core Beliefs has boosted the happiness and well-being of all three of the authors. We individually practice the concepts outlined in this book because of the benefits to our HEALTH, our EMOTIONS, our mental AWARENESS, our caring RELATIONSHIPS, and our TRANSCENDENCE through inspiring experiences. We have loving relationships with our partners, our children, our grandchildren, and our friends.

Do we live perfect lives? Absolutely not! We all have had health concerns, employment problems, and a lot of worries about members of our families. But despite the challenges we have faced, our lives are filled with hope and love.

As mental health professionals, we have had the opportunity to know many amazing individuals who have overcome trials, heartaches, and tragedies. Regardless of their circumstances, we have seen their courage and their resolve to move their lives forward by developing Positive Core Beliefs and improved Health Integration. Watching how they have made transformational changes encourages us to follow their examples. We are inspired by all who persist in building better lives for themselves and those they love through these fundamentals of Core-Related Health.

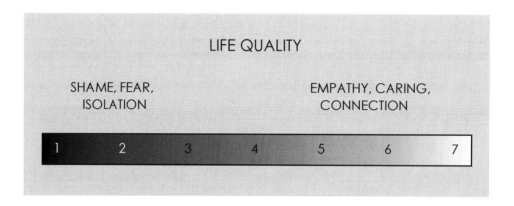

Many individuals have overcome shame, isolation, and fear through increased empathy, connection, and caring. Previously, some of them had lost all hope of having a purposeful and enjoyable life. But despite highly distressing circumstances, they surmounted what appeared to be impossible problems and then created new pathways for themselves.

The same possibilities are true for each of us. Very few of us escape trials or misfortunes. Despite our problems, we can continue to move forward. Our desire for better conditions produces options for our personal development and improved relationships.

It is our hope that each of our readers will constantly create added Positive Core Beliefs, an enriched Self-Belief Identity, and better HEART Health Integration. In this way, we can all draw on our Key Core Beliefs and gain the fullest measure of Core-Related Health.

CORE-RELATED HEALTH

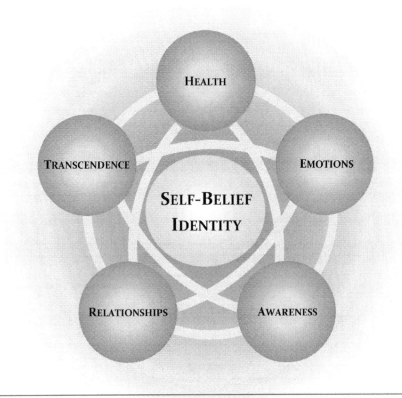

Don't stop here!
On the following pages you'll find a challenge to use
the principles you've learned in "KEY CORE BELIEFS"
as well as handy resources, including:

- ❏ A one-page, pull-out chart summarizing the concepts in this book (Appendix A, page 249),
- ❏ Suggestions for additional reading (Appendix B, page 251),
- ❏ How to find a qualified mental health professional (Appendix C, page 255),
- ❏ Notes for mental health professionals (Appendix D, page 257), and
- ❏ A list of the main concepts of "KEY CORE BELIEFS" (Appendix E, page 265).

We truly wish you all the best! *Gray, Sandi, and Jim*

NOTES:

Concluding Challenge

THE "KEY CORE BELIEFS" INVITATION

New Pathways for Enjoyable Living

We are what we desire to be.

Anonymous

HOW CAN I BEST USE THE PRINCIPLES OF "KEY CORE BELIEFS"?

Throughout the stages of our lives, we continually develop new Key Core Beliefs. As we grow older, additional self-beliefs arise at each of these stages. Our beliefs change during childhood (e.g. "I am a good reader"), teenage years (e.g. "I am unsure of myself"), young adulthood (e.g. "I am good-hearted"), middle age (e.g. "I am slowing"), and on into our later years (e.g. "Despite my age, I am healthy").

A runner who had completed several marathons in his 40s, realized in his 50s that he could no longer run eight-minute miles. At first this was disappointing and he believed, "I am slowing." He developed other beliefs including, "I am old," and "I am less competent." As he recognized that these age-related Negative Core Beliefs were unhelpful, he decided to look for more constructive alternatives. He soon realized that he enjoyed the competition in the over-50 age group. He then traded in his undesirable beliefs for new Positive Core Beliefs such as "I am passionately competitive," and "I may be older but I am ready for action!"

Becoming conscious of adverse beliefs is the first step in converting them into more truthful and supportive beliefs. Then we can consciously choose alternative Positive Core Beliefs. These beliefs will continue to strengthen our Self-Belief Identity.

THE "KEY CORE BELIEFS" INVITATION

The "KEY CORE BELIEFS" invitation encourages each of us to continue to be aware of any emerging Negative Core Beliefs and to develop beliefs that are accurate and inspiring.

Just like the runner described above, we all can create additional Positive Core Beliefs. By continually applying these Key Core Beliefs, we unlock greater health, more enjoyable relationships, and added meaning to our lives. This is our challenging opportunity.

Appendixes

"KEY CORE BELIEFS"

The Book Summarized
as a One-Page Chart

This chart summarizes the principles discussed in this book.
Feel free to make a copy as a reminder of how to pursue a fulfilling life.

BELIEVE

☐   Completely accept as true, "I am worthy to be loved."

☐   Persist in creating Positive Core Beliefs and Self-Belief Identity.

UNDERSTAND

Secondary Emotions:

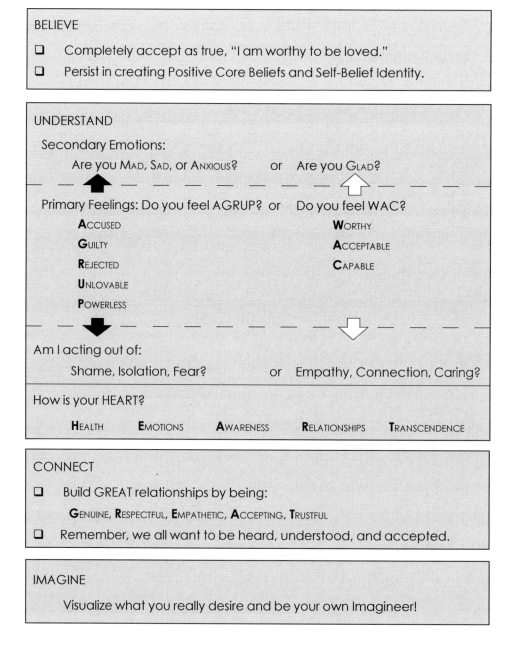

Are you MAD, SAD, or ANXIOUS?   or   Are you GLAD?

Primary Feelings: Do you feel AGRUP? or   Do you feel WAC?

ACCUSED	**W**ORTHY
GUILTY	**A**CCEPTABLE
REJECTED	**C**APABLE
UNLOVABLE	
POWERLESS	

Am I acting out of:

Shame, Isolation, Fear?   or   Empathy, Connection, Caring?

How is your HEART?

HEALTH   **E**MOTIONS   **A**WARENESS   **R**ELATIONSHIPS   **T**RANSCENDENCE

CONNECT

☐   Build GREAT relationships by being:

GENUINE, **R**ESPECTFUL, **E**MPATHETIC, **A**CCEPTING, **T**RUSTFUL

☐   Remember, we all want to be heard, understood, and accepted.

IMAGINE

Visualize what you really desire and be your own Imagineer!

ADDITIONAL READING

Other Authors Who Have Discussed Related Topics

The following books are part of a growing body of literature by authors who address how to create improved wellness and well-being. They offer innovative ways to better understand ourselves and others.

Brown, B. (2012). Daring greatly: How the courage to be vulnerable transforms the way we live, love, parent, and lead. New York, NY: Penguin Random House.

> Dr. Brené Brown has advanced the understanding of shame and the need for human connection, courage, compassion, and vulnerability in overcoming individual challenges. She is a noted writer and speaker and has been a featured presenter on TED talks.

Buettner, D. (2014). Blue Zones: 9 lessons for living longer. Washington, DC. National Geographic.

> In this book, Dan Buettner discusses the lifestyles of people who are healthy and live to be 100 years old in a number of zones around the world. These individuals take care of their health, regulate their emotions, maintain high degrees of mental resilience, enjoy close relationships, and engage in regular transcendent activities such as meditation, yoga, mindfulness, or spiritual traditions.

Fredrickson, B.L. (2009). Positivity. New York, NY: Crown.

> Dr. Barbara Fredrickson is a positive psychology researcher at the University of North Carolina. She studies the effects of positive emotions on personal resource-building and concludes that positive emotions promote new and creative actions, ideas, and social bonds.

Hannah, F. (2013). Pathways to mental health and anxiety management: An adventure into the mind. Palm Beach Gardens, FL: Retirement Investments, Inc.

> Frank Hannah, a mental health counselor, introduces the concept that mental health depends on the relationship between two factors in the brain: learned basic beliefs and four intrinsic behavioral goals. His book also explains how improved mental health reduces the occurrence of anxiety.

Johnson, S. (2008). Hold me tight: Seven conversations for a lifetime of love. New York, NY: Little, Brown and Company.

> Dr. Sue Johnson has written on topics related to couples' concerns. Her approach focuses on developing supportive dialogues between partners to further the bonds of their relationship with each other.

Lambrou, P. & Pratt, G. (2000). Acupressure for the emotions: Instant emotional healing. New York, NY: Broadway Books.

> Dr. Peter Lambrou and Dr. G. George Pratt, teach emotional self-management (ESM). Both are traditionally trained Psychologists with Cognitive Behavioral Therapy (CBT) backgrounds. ESM consists of self-administered, therapeutic tapping to alleviate anxiety and distress. This supports the formation of more positive perceptions of self.

Nathanson, D.L. (1992). Shame and pride: Affect, sex, and the birth of the self. New York, NY: W.W. Norton & Company, Inc.

> Dr. Donald Nathanson studied the influence of the brain and the role of emotions related to pride and shame. He defines the difference between shame and guilt, with shame relating to the quality of our person and guilt being the painful emotion that triggers compensatory actions.

Stosny, S. (2016). Soar above: How to use the most profound part of our brain under any kind of stress. Deerfield Beach, FL: Health Communications, Inc.

> Dr. Steven Stosny has studied how individuals can change their lives when they understand and regulate their emotions and then learn how to quit making the same patterns of mistakes. He explores the means to create added enjoyment through establishing effective coping mechanisms, being empowered, and building compassion.

FINDING A QUALIFIED MENTAL HEALTH PROFESSIONAL

Factors to Consider When Seeking a Counselor or Therapist

MENTAL HEALTH PROFESSIONALS WITH SPECIAL TRAINING

As noted in this book, some mental health professionals are specially trained to resolve traumatic and chronically distressful experiences. These specialists have a master's degree or a doctorate and are licensed in their state. Most of them have completed postgraduate training in treating trauma and anxiety. They may not use the specific approaches that are described in this book; however, they should be effective in helping people resolve trauma, anxiety, and depression, as well as any related Negative Core Beliefs.

If a person has a history of unresolved trauma, chronic distress, unexplained fears or phobias, anxiety, depression, or any other ongoing psychological concerns, he or she should consider seeing a mental health professional who specializes in alleviating the underlying causes of these conditions.

Mental health professionals who specialize in resolving these concerns will be happy to discuss their qualifications. Don't hesitate to ask any questions that will help you decide if a particular mental health professional will be effective for you. For example:

❑ Would you tell me about your education and postgraduate training?

❑ Do you have any special qualifications as a trauma specialist?

❑ Would you tell me what therapy approach you use to resolve PTSD and anxiety?

❑ How effective have you been in relieving distress for your former clients?

❑ How will I know if your work is effective for me?

❑ Would you provide the names of other mental health professionals with whom I could consult?

❑ Do you work with children, adolescents, adults, couples, and/or families?

❑ Other questions?

It is absolutely essential for the individual and the mental health professional to form a trusted and comfortable relationship. If this does not occur in the first few sessions, consider seeking help from another counselor or therapist.

NOTES FOR
MENTAL HEALTH
PROFESSIONALS

Applying the Concepts of "KEY CORE BELIEFS"
in Therapeutic Practice

THERAPEUTIC CONCEPTS FOR THE HEART OF A GREAT LIFE AND CORE-RELATED HEALTH

As noted in the copyright notice at the beginning of this book, the concepts expressed in this volume may be used by licensed mental health professionals in their practice. However, no part of this publication may be reproduced, stored, or transmitted. Additionally, no mental health professional or any other person may teach or present the concepts and ideas of this book, or any associated videos, programs, or materials to the public or other professionals unless they have been certified as a provider by Key Core Beliefs, Inc. Certification requirements can be viewed online at KeyCoreBeliefs.org. Written certification will be furnished to each authorized provider.

The concepts of "KEY CORE BELIEFS" can serve as a model to integrate client strengths with constructive experiences. These concepts are summarized and possible therapeutic applications are noted below.

1. BELIEVE: "I am worthy to be loved." Most individuals who have a substantial degree of depression or anxiety don't believe they are worthy of love. In many cases, this is the fundamental underlying reason for their distorted thoughts, feelings, and actions.

    ◊ Negative Core Beliefs commonly originate in traumatic or chronically distressful experiences that distort how individuals perceive themselves. These self-beliefs often lead to poor choices and behaviors as well as a deeply rooted sense of shame.

    ◊ Individuals who believe they are not worthy to be loved will often seek to accumulate evidence that their erroneous shame-based, Negative Core Beliefs are true.

    ◊ The psychic pain of shame dominates such individuals' sense of self, their Self-Belief Identity.

◊ Shamed-based Negative Core Beliefs are generally demonstrated through an individual's disparaging self-talk and harmful coping behaviors.

◊ Negative Core Beliefs are frequently the basis for the development of chronic depression and/or anxiety disorders.

THERAPEUTIC CONSIDERATIONS:

◊ Explore the individual's Negative Core Beliefs through inquiry: "What traumatic or chronically distressful experiences have you had?" "What are you ashamed of?" "What Negative Core Beliefs do you have about yourself, starting with the words, I am ... (e.g. "I am stupid," "I am unsafe," etc.).

◊ Distinguish the difference between guilt and shame ("I did something that was bad" or "That was an idiotic thing for me to do" [guilt] versus "I am bad" or "I am an idiot" [shame]).

◊ Help the individual convert Negative Core Beliefs into Positive Core Beliefs as illustrated in this book.

2. UNDERSTAND: Emotions, feelings, and self-regulation. Those afflicted with anxiety or depression often numb their painful emotions with compulsive, addiction-like behaviors.

◊ Many individuals feel flooded with unwanted emotions.

◊ Self-isolation often results in an increase of overwhelming emotions and feelings.

◊ Most individuals do not have a vocabulary to describe what they are experiencing. Therefore, the language of primary emotions—negative ones summarized by the AGRUP acronym (ACCUSED, GUILTY, REJECTED, UNLOVABLE, and/or POWERLESS) and positive ones summarized by the WAC acronym (WORTHY, ACCEPTABLE, and/or CAPABLE) can help them better understand their emotions.

THERAPEUTIC CONSIDERATIONS:

◊ Explain how to use an easy-to-understand emotional vocabulary.

◊ Distinguish secondary emotions ("I am mad") from primary feelings ("I feel ACCUSED, GUILTY, REJECTED, UNLOVABLE, and/or POWERLESS"—AGRUP) so the individual can identify and discuss their emotions and feelings.

◊ Focus on emotional experiences ("What emotions are you experiencing now?" "What are the underlying AGRUP feelings?")

◊ Help the individual learn principles of emotional intelligence, particularly how to regulate emotions.

Many individuals do not know how to perceive the balance needed for Health Integration and do not practice the HEART essentials (HEALTH, EMOTIONS, AWARENESS, RELATIONSHIPS, and TRANSCENDENCE). A review can help them better establish Health Integration.

ADDITIONAL THERAPEUTIC CONSIDERATIONS: HOW GOES YOUR HEART?

◊ How is your HEALTH? Review the following:

»   Schedule regular medical checkups

»   Rule out hormone imbalances (e.g. thyroid deficiency)

»   Practice good sleep hygiene; amount of sleep (7 to 8 hours a night)

»   Eat nutritiously

»   Limit alcohol, caffeine, soda, and sugar

»   Drink enough water

»   Exercise regularly

»   Quit smoking

»   Terminate the use of drugs and the misuse of prescription medications

»   Assess the individual's psychiatric and other medications

◊ How are your EMOTIONS?

> » Recognize emotions and feelings
> » Regulate and soothe yourself appropriately
> » Engage positively with others
> » Appreciate positive feelings and practice gratitude
> » Seek self-understanding
> » Draw on your capacity for empathy to understand others

◊ How is your AWARENESS?

> » Know what you focus on—are you aware of compulsive thoughts or behaviors?
> » Resolve shame and work through guilt
> » Value your worth and the worth of others
> » Realize that you are becoming more WAC—WORTHY, ACCEPTABLE, and CAPABLE.

◊ How are your RELATIONSHIPS?

> » Be responsible and accountable for your actions
> » Work through resentments
> » Forgive and be open to receiving forgiveness
> » Support the "five positive interactions to one negative" ratio
> » Act as an adult
> » Recognize whether you are acting in the role of an adult, a parent, or a child

◊ How is your TRANSCENDENT spirituality?

> » Develop your own sense of spiritual mindfulness
> » Tap into sources of positive energy
> » Practice meditation, prayer, or mindfulness
> » Learn how to discover the good things of life

3. CONNECT: Isolation is the common thread in anxiety and depression. Shame causes us to disconnect from others.

    ◊ The ability to connect with others leads each person to connect with self.

    ◊ Visualize new relationship strategies.

    ◊ When we better understand others through empathy, we overcome isolation.

THERAPEUTIC CONSIDERATIONS: BUILD GREAT RELATIONSHIPS

◊ Am I GENUINE? How much am I honest, sincere, open, and reliable so that others can completely trust me and be at ease with me?

◊ Am I RESPECTFUL? How much do I honor the rights of others to make their own choices and to be responsible for their decisions, even when I disagree with them?

◊ Am I EMPATHETIC? How much do I care about others—do I really listen to them and strive to understand their emotions, fears, and desires?

◊ Am I ACCEPTING? How much do I fully accept others as they are without imposing my expectations, values, judgments, or criticisms, even if I differ with them?

◊ Am I TRUSTFUL? How much do I believe in the good-hearted intentions of others—do I appreciate the best about them?

We all want to be heard. And understood. And accepted.

4. IMAGINE: When Walt Disney built Disneyland, he needed imaginative engineers. He called this capability "imagineering." Individuals can cultivate the ability to imagine their desires and then endeavor to fulfill them!

    ◊ Individuals with anxiety or depression expend little effort on obtaining enjoyment, meaning, or fulfillment.

    ◊ Those caught up in anxiety or depression may fear the responsibility as well as the opportunity to create their own life.

    ◊ In order to be fulfilled, it is crucial for individuals to visualize their life as satisfying and worthwhile.

THERAPEUTIC CONSIDERATIONS

◊ Each person can benefit by identifying his or her values.

◊ Individuals can achieve more of what they really want when they are aware of their most important desires. They will not find it effective merely to avoid what they do not want.

◊ Help individuals to imagine using the power of visualization and then engineer the creation of their desires on a daily basis.

THE CONCEPTS OF "KEY CORE BELIEFS"

1. Core-Related Health depends on two fundamentals:

    ◊ A Self-Belief Identity based on predominantly Positive Core Beliefs

    ◊ Health Integration that includes the five HEART essentials (HEALTH, EMOTIONS, AWARENESS, RELATIONSHIPS, and TRANSCENDENCE).

2. Transforming Negative Core Beliefs into Positive Core Beliefs can effectively resolve trauma and chronic distress.

3. Individuals can work through their underlying sources of shame.

4. The five HEART essentials of Health Integration serve as a model that individuals can use to create comprehensive physical wellness and emotional well-being.

5. By practicing the GREAT interpersonal skills (being GENUINE, RESPECTFUL, EMPATHETIC, ACCEPTING, and TRUSTFUL), individuals will achieve better interpersonal outcomes and improved relationships.

6. Positive reinforcement occurs as a natural result of applying the principles outlined in "KEY CORE BELIEFS."

7. Each of us can develop the Positive Core Beliefs that will strengthen our Self-Belief Identity, and we can also increase Health Integration to obtain greater Core-Related Health.